Praise for *A Teen's Guide to the 5 Love Languages*

A Teen's Guide to the 5 Love Languages is brilliantly written, easy to comprehend, and simple to apply to your relationships.

ZACK, 16

Understanding how to give and receive love well is foundational for healthy relationships. I would have greatly appreciated a book like this when I was a teenager. Even now as I am in my twenties, I found this book to be very helpful and I can only imagine the positive effect it would have had on my relationships in my teenage years. Gary Chapman's insights address the need in all of us to feel known and connected. His writing is also very practical and relevant to teens.

KATHRYN, 23

This book gave me a better understanding of my relationships. I've already used it to become closer with one of my friends who, because of this book, is now my best friend.

MELANIA, 16

This was an easy-to-read book that helped me understand what my love language is and how to better love others by understanding theirs.

LUKE, 13

As a teacher I am excited to use this text in my classroom to help teach our Relationship Unit. I strongly believe that this is going to make such an impact on my students' lives. This is something they can start applying from day one that will last a lifetime!

MARY, 27

D0965401

This book really clarified not only my own personality, but also that of my siblings and friends. I found super practical ways to love those around me!

REBEKAH, 17

I give this book a five-star review! It is incredibly helpful! After learning my love language and those of my parents, we knew how to show love to each other better and show that we care more. This book gives great details explaining each of the love languages with descriptive examples and stories that are incredibly relatable to any teenager. I would recommend this book to anyone that is seeking to be a better friend, daughter, son, sibling, or student.

HANNAH, 15

A Teen's Guide to the 5 Love Languages was excellently done. I learned not only about my friends and family, but also about myself. I loved the way it was written. It was a quick, easy, and informative read.

MYKALA, 18

A TEEN'S GUIDE TO THE 5 LOVE LANGUAGES®

HOW TO UNDERSTAND YOURSELF AND IMPROVE
ALL YOUR RELATIONSHIPS

WRITTEN BY **GARY CHAPMAN** WITH PAIGE HALEY DRYGAS

NORTHFIELD PUBLISHING

CHICAGO

Edited by Pam Pugh
Interior and Cover Design: Erik M. Peterson
Illustrations: © 2016 by Paul Crouse

Produced in association with Hudson Bible

Library of Congress Cataloging-in-Publication Data

Names: Chapman, Gary D., author. | Drygas, Paige, author.
Title: A teen's guide to the 5 love languages : how to understand yourself
   and improve all your relationships / Gary Chapman, with
   Paige Haley Drygas.
Other titles: Teen's guide to the five love languages
Description: Chicago, IL : Northfield Publishing, [2016] | Includes
   bibliographical references.
Identifiers: LCCN 2015043141 | ISBN 9780802414359
Subjects: LCSH: Interpersonal communication in adolescence--Juvenile
   literature. | Interpersonal relations in adolescence--Juvenile literature.
   | Interpersonal communication--Religious aspects--Christianity--Juvenile
   literature. | Interpersonal relations--Religious
   aspects--Christianity--Juvenile literature.
Classification: LCC BF724.3.I55 .C43 2016 | DDC 155.5/19--dc23 LC record available at http://
lccn.loc.gov/2015043141

We hope you enjoy this book from Northfield Publishing. Our goal is to provide high-quality, thought-provoking books and products that connect truth to your real needs and challenges. For more information on other books and products that will help you with all your important relationships, go to 5lovelanguages.com or write to:

Northfield Publishing
820 N. LaSalle Blvd.
Chicago, IL 60610

5 7 9 10 8 6 4

Printed in the United States of America

*Dedicated to all teenagers who want to invest their lives
in making the world a better place*

CONTENTS

WELCOME TO 5LL

The book you're holding in your hands might be one of the simplest, most commonsense, profound, life-transforming books you've ever held.

That's what's amazing about *The 5 Love Languages*. When you read it, you'll nod and think, *Yes, that makes total sense. Why didn't I think of that before?* And you'll discover, as millions of other readers have before you, that this simple concept can transform your relationships.

Think about that in fast-forward through your life. By learning the 5LL now, over time you'll have

- tighter bonds with your friends;
- better communication with your parents;
- closer relationships with your siblings;
- dating relationships with less drama and awkwardness;
- a healthier marriage someday;
- a clearer understanding of interpersonal dynamics and human motivation.

And you'll save yourself loads of conflict, dysfunction, grief, and stress.

At the heart of the 5LL concept is this idea: **All of us want to be known and loved. That's universal. However, *how* we want to be loved is unique to each of us.**

So like all the best inventions on the planet—pepperoni pizza, the iPhone, Frappuccinos, and Instagram—5LL is intuitive. Clear. Life altering. Ready to read on?

– Paige Haley Drygas

GETTING STARTED

HOW MANY LANGUAGES DO YOU SPEAK?

Drew and Emily seem really happy together, but will they last? It's too soon to tell. For their ten-month anniversary, Emily wrote a list of the top ten things she loves about Drew. She created a mini-book filled with thoughtful words and ideas. Em worked really hard on the project.

For Emily, Drew gave her ten little gifts that tied to ten of their most memorable dates from their months together, like a Braves pennant, a set of ceramic chopsticks, specialty trampoline socks, and pepper spray for hiking. Drew put a lot of thought into those ten gifts.

And they both felt disappointed.

Do you spot the disconnect? Emily's drawn to Words, so she expressed her love for Drew with words. Gifts mean a lot to Drew, so he expressed his love for Emily with gifts. They both wanted to please the other, but they weren't speaking each other's languages. They invested a lot of effort, but effort alone doesn't make someone feel loved.

It's time for Drew and Emily to learn another language.

Are you studying a foreign language? Maybe you're in the throes of conjugating French verbs or memorizing Latin roots or practicing your Spanish phrases. The really ambitious students tackle multiple foreign languages and throw a non-Romance language, like Mandarin Chinese, into the mix.

Studying a foreign language can be grueling, but imagine if you'd simply grown up in a bilingual home. (Maybe you did, lucky you.) Speaking two languages would seem as natural as breathing. Or rather than starting with a Spanish textbook in high school, imagine if you'd started in a Spanish immersion program in kindergarten, with a teacher chatting to you in Spanish for thirty minutes a day. Like a sponge, you'd absorb the language; you'd become fluent.

Learning a new language takes work, time, and patience. You can't sleep with a French textbook for a pillow and wake up thinking *en français*.

In the same way, in order to speak nonnative emotional languages, we have to train our minds. It doesn't happen through osmosis or happy thinking. **Without being fluent in the love languages, our relationships will suffer, causing friction with those closest to us—our friends, parents, siblings, boyfriend or girlfriend, mentors, coaches, and so on.** You get the picture—lower fluency, higher friction; higher fluency, lower friction. This could be an ongoing source of stress in your life or an incredible opportunity to thrive in your relationships.

It's time to learn a new language.

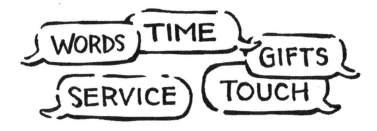

FIVE EMOTIONAL LANGUAGES

Sometimes teachers make you dig for the thesis of a book, like a warped treasure hunt. Instead, I'll wrap this thesis in flashing Christmas lights for you. This comes from years of counseling experience.

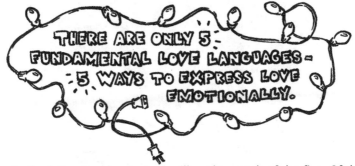

THERE ARE ONLY 5 FUNDAMENTAL LOVE LANGUAGES — 5 WAYS TO EXPRESS LOVE EMOTIONALLY.

In the following chapters we will explore each of the five. Of the five love languages, each of us has a primary language—a way of receiving devotion and affection that registers deep inside and makes us feel truly, personally loved. One of the five speaks more deeply to us emotionally than the other four. We can receive love through all five, but if we don't receive our primary love language, then we will not *feel* loved, even though the person is speaking some combination of the other four. However, if someone speaks our primary love language sufficiently, then the other four are just bonus.

THE RIGHT LANGUAGE

Here's the challenge: by nature, we tend to speak our own love language. That is, we express love to others in the language that would make us feel loved. But if it is not their primary love language, it will not mean to them what it would mean to us.

It's like the clueless traveler who shows up in a foreign country. He only speaks one language (his own), so to communicate with "the foreigners" (wait a second—*he's* the foreigner in this story), he speaks loudly and slowly, as if shouting will help him communicate. It's such a sad, comical scene.

The same thing happens all the time in emotional communication. Let's say your sister's primary love language is Service, so she constantly finds creative ways to serve you. She gives you the biggest slice of pizza, carries your backpack into the mudroom, stays up late to help you with your science fair project. Meanwhile, let's say your primary language is Words, so you send her encouraging messages and brag about her to your friends. You're both loving each other, but you're each speaking your own language. Disconnect! If you'd simply vacuum her car for her one day, that would mean more to her than all your words combined.

Scenarios like this play out in millions of relationships. Each person speaks his or her own language and does not understand why the other does not feel loved. If we want the other person to feel loved, we must discover and learn to speak *their* primary love language. It's time to work smarter, not harder, and to translate love into the language the other will naturally receive.

THE NO-LOGIC ZONE

Logic might suggest that we naturally gravitate toward people who share our primary love language. We might (falsely) assume that Service people date other Service people (because they shovel each other's driveways) or that all the Time students try out for the swim team (because they're the only ones who make time for early morning practices). Or that Touch is contagious in a family, so they all must go around hugging one another constantly. We might (falsely) think that people with common interests and ties share the same love language and communicate their affection easily and freely, forever and ever, amen.

Does your family run on logic? Or your friendships? Or any relationship, for that matter? No, we love our people because they're our people.

The truth is that in any collection of people, you'll find a mix of love languages. One friend who's built up by Words is drawn to another friend who appreciates Gifts. One person who experiences love through Time marries a partner whose love language is Touch. And surprise, surprise, their kids have love languages all their own.

And a language barrier is created.

Even those rare pairs who share a primary love language find that there are countless distinct "dialects" within each language. No two people express and receive love in exactly the same way. We're individuals with custom languages all our own.

Does that seem like a recipe for failure? Or proof of the old expression "opposites attract"? Diversity in relationships makes us stronger and makes life more interesting. How boring would it be if you and all your friends had identical thoughts and tastes? Language barriers don't have to stunt your relationships. Think about pro sports teams, like in the English Premier League or NHL.

Their players often speak three (or more) different languages, yet they *find* ways to communicate. You can too.

THIS IS UNIVERSAL

Everyone reading this book has relationships. The question is this: what is the quality of those relationships? Positive and affirming relationships bring us great satisfaction, but negative and draining relationships bring us deep pain. **Is it too bold to suggest that life's greatest happiness is found in good relationships and life's deepest hurt is found in bad relationships?**

The five love languages apply in *all* human relationships. They're universal. Some people never feel loved by their parents, not because their parents do not love them, but because their parents never learned to speak their primary love language. Other people struggle in team settings, not because they aren't talented, but because they've never learned to express appreciation to their teammates. They unwittingly communicate to their coaches and teammates, "I don't need you; you're not valuable to me." This strains the relationships and tanks the team's success. Still other people struggle to make lasting friendships. Their friends feel unappreciated, unloved, and unknown.

Learning to speak love and appreciation in a language the other person can receive is the key to enhancing all human relationships.

If you read the following chapters and apply the principles of the five love languages, you will become more effective in *all* your relationships. These principles are the same truths I have shared with hundreds of clients in my counseling office. These are for you too.

OUR PARENTS

All our relationships are shaped by our relationships with our parents. These are primal, original bonds. If you feel loved by your mom, then the maternal relationship brings you a feeling of comfort and encouragement. On the other hand, if your relationship with your mom is fractured, then you likely suffer feelings of abandonment. And if you were abused by your mom, then you feel hurt and anger, maybe even hatred.

Lack of parental love often motivates children to go searching for love in other relationships. This misguided search often leads to further disappointment.

Whether you like it or not, all your relationships spring from the relationship you have with your parents. The nature of that relationship will color all other relationships, so it's important to be aware of what has worked—and hasn't—in your relationship with your parents.

LOVE VS. ROMANCE

Of course, these principles also apply to your romantic relationships (current, healthy, dying, nonexistent, pending, future, all of the above). First let's land this rocket on Planet Reality.

Our culture is addicted to romantic love. Want evidence? Just listen to our songs and watch our movies. Yet oddly, we're also very ignorant about love. We have bought into the story line that love is something that magically happens to you. If you have it, you have it; if you don't, you don't. That's a simplistic view of love. We need a robust, realistic view of what romantic love really looks like.

At first, falling in love is an obsessive, addictive adrenaline rush. During this early stage of love, which may last a year or two, we live under the illusion that the other person is perfect—or at least perfect for us. Even if our friends can see the other person's flaws, we're blind to them. During this phase, we have irrational thoughts, such as, "I'll never be happy without this person. Nothing else in life really matters." Carried away by these thoughts, we make rash choices, like dropping out of our favorite activities to be with the other person. In this stage of love, we *feel* more than we *think*; we're magnetically drawn to the other person. We assume we'll live happily ever after. At the beginning, love is effortless. We don't work to fall in love—it just happens.

But real romantic love has another stage. Once we come down from the high of the obsessive stage, long-term relationships require real, hard work, which is why understanding the five love languages is so critical to keeping love alive.

In this next stage of love, the blind obsession begins to fade, and the illusions of perfection evaporate. Our differences become obvious. The partner who feels loved by Gifts lavishes thoughtful presents on the other person, while the Words person pours out verbal love. Neither feels loved, and emotional distance grows. Each person's love tank—the personal reservoir of feeling genuinely adored, appreciated, and known—starts to empty. This often happens in long-term relationships. Some couples settle for the leftovers, disappointed by the fizzle. Others allow their unmet needs to fester and spark conflicts. Some suffer in silence, each blaming the other. Some convince themselves they're stuck with the wrong person.

Can such a tarnished relationship be reborn? Yes—but only if the couple learns how to express love in a language the other person can receive. Lasting love requires hard work through conscious, intentional, thoughtful choices. **Love isn't a feeling; it's an action.**

The word *love* can be used as a noun ("They're in *love*") or a verb ("They *love* each other"). For our purposes, we'll consider *love* an action word—showing and receiving love, doing something for someone. With realistic expectations of love and practice expressing it, our present and future relationships will thrive.

love tank : noun 1.PERSONAL RESERVOIR 2.OF FEELING ADORED, APPRECIATED, KNOWN 3.WHICH EMPTIES WHEN FEELING UNLOVED 4.WHICH FILLS WHEN FEELING LOVED

AN OPPORTUNITY

You might feel like you're starting from scratch, and that's okay. You might have to unlearn some bad habits you've developed in your relationships. The process might feel awkward at first. If you're a Service person, then giving Time to someone might feel unnatural or forced at first. Little by little, though, that will change. With repetition and the right attitude, you'll see growth in your relationships. **By learning the love languages, you'll make a lasting difference in the lives of those you love.**

5LL TIPS FOR TODAY

1. Fresh Start
Did you fail yesterday? Today is a new day. Cut yourself some slack, and start again.

2. Vision
Look with fresh eyes at your relationships. Truly see the individuals and their needs. Spot new opportunities to show your love.

3. Experimentation
Try something new or unconventional. Be creative. If A worked yesterday, mix in some B and C today.

4. Teachability

Proud Payton thinks she's already a relational expert. Humble Hunter is constantly learning, asking for advice from role models, and looking for ideas from healthy relationships. Be open to learning!

5. Endurance

If at first you don't succeed . . . give up? No! Your relationships are worth the investment, so keep going and growing. Life is a wild journey.

PAUSE & PROCESS

1. Our culture often dilutes the meaning of the word *love*—we tend to use the same word for how we feel about Belgian waffles or a football team that we use to describe our deepest bonds. ("I love waffles! I love the Packers! I love you!") How would you define the word *love*?

2. Why is *love* better understood as a verb than as a noun?

3. Which of your relationships would you describe as healthy?

4. Which of your relationships would you like to see improved?

5. How would you describe your relationship with your mom? Your dad? How might your relationships with them affect your other relationships?

6. In your own words, how could learning to speak the five love languages enrich your relationships?

7. What makes you feel truly loved? Do you have a hunch yet on which is your primary love language?

8. Who in your life loves you unconditionally?

CHAPTER 1

LOVE LANGUAGE #1: WORDS

Gemma didn't say much. She didn't have to. Her actions spoke for themselves. When she took the field, she worked harder than anyone else. Which was shocking, because she was the best player.

But when Gemma spoke, everyone listened. The whole team respected her. Meghan said, "I remember one game when I was struggling, so distracted by this fight I'd had with my friend and this massive history project I had due the next day. I wasn't playing well. At half-time Gemma pulled me off to the side and quietly said, 'You're better than this, Meghan. I know you can beat your player.' Just the way she said it, so confident in me, it made me believe in myself. So I stepped up and played solidly the rest of the game."

Gemma's words had that effect. The team made it to the state finals that year. Gemma was only a sophomore then, but she told the team, "We're faster and smarter. We can beat this team." And they did.

Maybe if she'd been one of those players who talks constantly or blames others for every little error, the other players would have tuned her out. Instead they listened. They took her words to heart.

We're all native speakers of one language: selfishness. From the time we were little kids, we saw ourselves as the center of the universe. It comes so naturally to us to think and talk about ourselves incessantly.

But in order to grow in our relationships, we have to learn a new language: Words of Affirmation. We have to speak life-giving words, positive words, true and confident words that build others up. Many of the people in our lives crave *words,* and it's up to us to learn how to speak them.

"The tongue has the power of life and death,"[1] a wise man once said. Bold claim, right? But think of how you've experienced that to be true in your own life.

Can you recall a time when someone said something really hurtful to you—personal, mocking, or cutting words—that made you feel small and doubt yourself? Sadly, we often remember those words our whole lives.

In contrast, can you also recall a time when someone said something really kind and memorable to you—something personal and encouraging from someone who saw potential in you, maybe potential you didn't even know you had?

Then you know the life-and-death power of words. **The right words spoken at the right time by the right person can inspire you to do and be more.** It's this potential for good that makes Words such a powerful love language.

words of affirmation: *noun*
1. TRUTHFUL WORDS 2. SPOKEN OR WRITTEN
3. FROM ONE PERSON TO ANOTHER 4. TO
UPLIFT OR ENCOURAGE 5. TO MAKE THE
RECIPIENT FEEL LOVED

My goal for you is that you will learn to both *receive* and *give* love in all five love languages. It seems fair to assume that anyone who takes the time to read this book wants to become a better person and have deeper relationships. Learning the five love languages will help you do both.

The good news is that all these languages can be learned. For some people, Words is their primary love language (especially if they grew up with a really verbal parent), but all of us need to be able to speak it, and all of us enjoy hearing positive words. So how can we best develop this language?

LISTENING AND RECEIVING

We'll spend more of the chapter focusing on how to give Words of Affirmation, but a quick note before we do.

You have to know how to receive Words of Affirmation too.

When someone you know, respect, and love says something specific *to* you *about* you, listen closely.

- When a teacher affirms, "Of course I marked things for you to work on, but I'm so impressed by the level of original thought in your writing."
- When a coach says, "Our entire team relies on your determination. Your will to win sets the tone for the whole game."
- When a mentor says, "I'm seeing so much growth in you. Last fall you were struggling with _____, but you've conquered that and are in a completely different place now."
- When a parent says, "I really enjoy hanging out with you. You're an interesting conversationalist."
- When a friend says, "I knew I could call you. I knew you'd be there for me."

Rather than blowing off those Words of Affirmation with a self-deprecating comment or some sarcasm to deflect the attention away from you, accept the words. Soak them in. Listen for the specific feedback you're receiving, and accept the love you're being given.

THINKING AND GIVING

Think about the power of your words. For people whose primary love language is Words, compliments and encouragement aren't just empty gestures or polite conversation techniques. They're soul food.

People don't just hear this:

- "Well done!"
- "You look really good."
- "Wow, I'm impressed with you."

They also hear what you mean behind those words:

- "You have value."
- "I love you."
- "You're important to me."

The real power of words lies in their ability to fill people's love tanks. Through specific, intentional things you say, you can fill people up.

How do you feel about that kind of power? That might depend on your own primary love language. For some people, it feels awkward at first to say Words of Affirmation. For others, especially those who grew up in really verbal homes, it might feel more natural. But not only can you learn this language, you can also become fluent in it.

WARNING: SKIP THE FLATTERY

Flattery is not a dialect of the Words love language; flattery is the language of manipulation. Flatterers have an agenda. Ultimately they want to get something from the person they're flattering. Flattery lacks one key ingredient: sincerity. You can tell when someone's faking—it's so obvious. Right after the fake compliment comes the request, like this: "Mom, you're the best mom ever! Can I go over to my friend's house tonight?" (Cue the eye rolls.) Twisting Words of Affirmation to get something is wrong, and it wrecks trust. The person being flattered realizes you aren't being honest with your words and becomes suspicious of you. That person starts to wonder, *Can I even trust what this person says?* Most people don't like to be friends with flatterers.

Unlike shallow flattery, Words of Affirmation run deep. They're rooted in intimate knowledge of the person you're affirming. While flattery makes people feel suspicious or defensive, sincere words make people feel safe and known.

// WARNING: BAN HARASSMENT // Students can be brutal to one another. "Sticks and stones may break my bones, but words will never hurt me." Remember that old saying? It's a lie. Words do hurt, sometimes worse than a physical injury. While a broken bone may heal completely, hurtful words may stay with us for life. **Words leave the mouth, travel to the ears, and lodge straight in the heart—often forever.** We have to be very careful with what we say.

Every love language has an opposite. Just as a love language has the potential to do immense good, the opposite of a love language has the potential to inflict serious harm. The opposite of using Words of Affirmation as a love language is using words to put someone down. The severe form of this is harassment, which is when one person or group calls another person names and puts them down again and again.

Legally, harassment encompasses a lot more than just mean words. It can also include physically harming another student or his property, interfering with a student's education, creating a threatening educational environment, disrupting the orderly conduct of the school, making a threatening phone call, or sending a threatening text or email.

Everyone deserves to feel safe, which includes not experiencing harassment. If you are being harassed or know of someone being harassed, tell someone. Today.

Reporting is not the same as tattling. Tattling is for the purpose of getting someone in trouble. Little kids are experts at this tactic. Reporting protects someone's safety and is essential to a healthy environment.

DIALECTS

Back to positive words. Words of Affirmation is one of the five basic love languages. Within that one language are several different dialects. (Think of London, Sydney, Dallas, Boston, Charleston—people in these places all speak English, but they don't sound anything alike. Right, y'all?)

Words of Appreciation

Through words of appreciation, we express sincere gratitude for some act of service rendered. We say "thanks" to someone specific for something specific. This means so much to the people who serve us silently, often thanklessly, day in and day out.

Your parents, for example. How many meals have they cooked for you over the years? Loads of laundry? Personal sacrifices? Putting your needs before their own? And yes, they do that because they're your parents and they love you, but can you imagine how much it would mean to them to hear some genuine thanks?

- "Mom [or Dad], thanks for coming to my concert."
- "Thanks for buying my favorite cereal."
- "Thanks for letting me use the car."
- "Thanks for working hard so we can go on vacation."

It doesn't take a ton of creativity or thought or effort. Just a little observation and a sincere sentence or two of thanks.

Same goes for your teachers, coaches, pastors. Your coach could be making a lot more money doing something else but sacrifices countless hours to invest in you. Your teachers work in a culture of bureaucracy and complaining yet find the energy to dream up a new project for your class.

Not often do they hear even a passing "thanks"—so think about what your words of appreciation could mean to someone who serves you.

Words of Encouragement

To *encourage* literally means "to inspire courage" in someone, to make someone feel more hopeful or confident. All of us feel insecure or lack courage about something. That insecurity and fear can hold us back from doing what we'd like to do.

Maybe you see some latent potential in a friend or sibling, and all that person needs is a little dose of encouragement from you.

- "You should try out for the play. I could totally see you in that role."
- "Have you considered running cross-country? You could do it."

Encourage them to explore their desire or give it a try. That might be the nudge they need to try something new.

PICTURE ME: I WAS THE SILENT KID WHO SAT IN THE BACK OF THE CLASSROOM, THE DARK AND BROODING TYPE. I WAS AN AVERAGE STUDENT AT BEST, AND I DIDN'T PARTICULARLY LIKE ENGLISH CLASS. I DIDN'T THINK I WAS A GOOD WRITER BECAUSE I WASN'T GOOD WITH THE MECHANICS, LIKE SPELLING AND COMMAS.

AND THEN I MET MRS. DOMINGUEZ. SHE WAS MY SOPHOMORE LIT TEACHER. SHE SAW SOMETHING IN ME. MY PAPERS DIDN'T COME BACK LOOKING LIKE THEY WERE BLEEDING, WITH RED INK MARKING ALL MY MISTAKES. THEY CAME BACK WITH LITTLE NOTES TO ME.

"TOM, YOU HAVE A GIFT."

"TOM, YOUR THOUGHTS ARE DEEP AND ORIGINAL."

"TOM, YOU ARE A WRITER."

THIS WAS A FIRST FOR ME. MRS. D. OPENED MY EYES TO A TALENT I DIDN'T EVEN KNOW I HAD.

I'VE BEEN ACCEPTED AT NORTHWESTERN FOR NEXT YEAR. GUESS WHAT I WANT TO STUDY?

WRITING.

—TOM

Sometimes our friends feel us out to see how we'll respond. A friend might say, "I was thinking of running for student council, but I just don't know." Will you brush off the comment by saying, "It's just a popularity contest. It's not worth your time"? Will you discourage your friend by saying, "I don't know. That's a lot of work, and it's so hard to win"? Or will you speak some words of encouragement, such as, "I'd love to hear your ideas for why you want to run. Need a campaign manager?"

Words of Praise

To some extent, all of us are achievers. We set goals we hope to accomplish, and when we do, we like to be recognized. As the Oscars are to Hollywood, as the Grammys are to the music scene, as trophies are to winning athletes, and even the plaque at a local restaurant is to the employee of the month—so words of praise meet the need for recognition in personal relationships.

Our culture is fluent in criticism. We excel at pointing out what's wrong in 140 characters or less. We've mastered the art of cynicism as well as the habit of sarcasm.

It takes more discipline and creativity to see what's right—and to say it. "You did really well at _____." All around us are people who deserve a little credit: a friend who survived her parents' divorce without getting bitter; a friend who's overcome a serious health issue yet always thinks of others; an older brother who just finished college; a little sister who read the whole Harry Potter series despite her dyslexia; a boyfriend who comes back from an ACL surgery and makes the varsity team.

All around us are quiet heroes, champions who never make the headlines but who deserve a lot of credit. They need to hear our words of praise.

Words of Kindness

What we say matters a lot; *how* we say it matters just as much, if not more. Sometimes our words are saying one thing but our tone of voice is saying another. That's a double message. People usually interpret our meaning based on our tone of voice, not only the words we use.

If your friend says in a sarcastic tone, "I would love to go running with you on the lakefront path," you won't hear a genuine invitation in those words. ("Ummm . . . no thanks," you'd reply.)

On the other hand, you can hear even a hard message if it's delivered in a kind tone: "I felt disappointed that you didn't invite me to go running with you." In this case, the person speaking wants to be known by the other person and is trying to build authenticity into their relationship. (The natural response: "I'm sorry, I didn't realize you wanted to go. Want to run together tomorrow?")

How we speak is so important. An ancient sage once said, "A gentle answer turns away wrath."[2] When a friend lashes out at you verbally, if you answer gently, the heat simmers down. You'll be able to hear what the person is saying, empathize, apologize if needed, or calmly explain your perspective. You won't assume your point of view is the only way to interpret what's happened. That response shows maturity. Mature love speaks kindly.

FORGIVENESS

In order to speak affirming words, we have to process our hurt and anger in healthy ways. Our words are an overflow of our hearts. If hurt and anger are festering in our hearts, then we will naturally come out fighting, verbally destroying rather than loving others.

Many people mess up each new day with what happened yesterday. They insist on dragging into the present the failures of the past; in doing so, they pollute the present and the future. When bitterness, resentment, and a thirst for revenge grow unchecked in the human heart, words of affirmation will be nearly impossible to speak.

Enter forgiveness. Yes, the injury happened. Certainly it hurt and may still hurt. Forgiveness doesn't make it okay; it makes *you* okay. You can choose to release the hurt and anger so you are no longer consumed by them. You can choose to love people despite the harm they inflicted, while setting healthy boundaries to protect yourself in the future. Forgiveness allows you to live your life in peace.

Sometimes the person will acknowledge her failure; sometimes she won't. Either way, you can choose to forgive and to release that person to God, who will make all things right in the end. You can refuse to allow the other person's choices to wreck your life.

And when you're the one who inflicted the wound, you can ask this loving question: "What can I do to make up for the pain I caused you?" You can't erase the past, but you can confess it, agree that it was wrong, and ask for forgiveness. Only then does reconciliation become a possibility.

Unforgiveness will seep out in your words. Harsh, condemning words erode relationships. Words of affirmation enhance relationships.

Remember, love is a choice; love is an action word.

WORDS QUIZ

How word-savvy are you? Check the phrases that are genuine Words of Affirmation. Place an X next to lousy things to say.

_____ "It wasn't the worst meal I've ever eaten."

_____ "Absolutely, I think you should try out for the spring play. I think you'd be perfect in that role."

_____ "Everyone, you're all so amazing! You're the best people in the history of the world!"

_____ "I'm reading a book that tells me to compliment people, so I just wanted to tell you that you're decent at baseball."

_____ "Sure, you look fine."

_____ "That blue shirt looks fantastic with your eyes."

_____ "Thanks for listening. You're such a good friend."

_____ "Do you realize how natural you are with kids? Have you ever considered being a teacher? I think you'd be really good at it."

_____ "Thanks for driving me to all my rehearsals, Mom. I know they're at
weird times."

_____ "Well, at least you get credit for trying."

_____ "You've become such a dangerous attacker. I'm so glad you're on my
team."

_____ "I'm so proud of you. I know you hate public speaking, but you gave a
solid presentation."

PAUSE & PROCESS

1. To what degree have you received Words of Affirmation from your parents?

2. Do you find it easy or difficult to speak Words of Affirmation to your family? Why?

3. How freely do you express Words of Affirmation in other relationships?

4. What are words that have been spoken to you that made you feel loved?

5. Of the five love languages, most people have one favorite that makes them feel most loved. Identifying your primary love language can feel confusing, because everyone likes all five languages. (Who doesn't like to hear kind words, for example?) Personal application: Are Words your primary love language—do they make you feel especially good or loved?

6. Make a list of your primary relationships—not every single friend or acquaintance but those closest to you (two to ten names). Is Words the love language of one of your people?

7. Review the dialects of Words (appreciation, encouragement, praise, and kindness). If one of your people is nourished by words, then script something to say that would make that person feel loved.

8. Practice speaking the dialect of appreciation to someone who's rarely thanked, such as a parent or teacher. Say something simple, kind, and truthful to that person today.

9. Unforgiveness seeps out in your words. Are you harboring unforgiveness toward someone? What can you do to address it and release the person?

CHAPTER 2

LOVE LANGUAGE #2: TIME

If your sister invites you to go see a movie with her, it could be that she's really interested in that movie, or it could be that she just wants to spend time with you. If her love language is Time, then the activity of choice isn't significant—trade meeting for coffee or going on a bike ride for watching a movie and she's just as happy.

What matters is the time together. That can be a hard lesson to learn for people who have other love languages. For example, a Gifts person might show up at the theater with a box of her sister's favorite candy and then dash out as soon as the movie ends. A Words person might fill up the car ride with words and then text friends during the movie. A Service person might show up to the movie late because he was busy dropping off his sister's overdue library books. A Touch person might give his sister a bear hug and then fall asleep during the previews.

And all these well-meaning people would miss the point. **The person who craves Time just wants *you*: your time, your attention, your company.** Many of us are so task oriented that we can't even fathom the idea of slowing down and giving someone the old-fashioned, priceless gift of time, but for many people, that's precisely what makes them feel loved.

People who crave Time want togetherness. That's not the same as proximity. Two people can be in close proximity and ignore each other completely, as if the other doesn't exist. Being together involves giving someone your focused, undivided attention. As humans, we have a fundamental need to connect with others. We may be surrounded by other people all day long, but that doesn't mean we feel connected.

"We are all so much together, but we are all dying of loneliness."

—Albert Schweitzer

When Time is used to express genuine love, it communicates powerfully on the emotional level. If you throw a Frisbee, kick a soccer ball, or bounce on a trampoline with your younger sibling, that kid receives the gift of your time. For those moments, whether it's an hour or even just five minutes, you are together. If, however, you're checking Facebook while spending time "together," then your sibling doesn't have your undivided attention—and won't feel loved.

Quality Time does not mean we must spend all our moments gazing deeply into each other's eyes or doing everything with the same friend. Spending time together means doing something we both enjoy. The particular activity is secondary, only a means to creating the sense of togetherness.

quality time : *adjective + noun*
1. INTENTIONAL 2. DELIBERATE TIME 3. SPENT WITH A PERSON 4. TO MAKE THE INDIVIDUAL FEEL LOVED

The important thing about bouncing on the trampoline with your little brother or sister isn't the physical act of jumping but the emotions created between you. Same with friends who play tennis together: if their goal is Time, then what happens on the emotional level is what matters. They may not ace every serve or qualify for Wimbledon, but by spending time together on a common interest, they communicate that they care about each other and enjoy just being together.

DIALECT #1: QUALITY CONVERSATION

Remember how Words of Affirmation had many dialects? So does Quality Time.

One of the most common dialects is quality conversation.

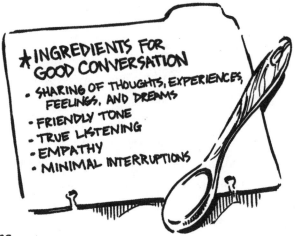

Hearing

Whereas affirming words depend on what we are *saying* (the content), quality conversation focuses on what we are *hearing* (truly listening to and understanding the other person). If I'm showing love for you with Quality Time, and we're spending that time in conversation, then I will focus on drawing you out by actively listening to what you're saying. I will ask questions, not in a badgering style, but with a genuine desire to understand how you think and feel.

After dating Jacob for three months, Olivia finally told him that she wished he weren't so attached to his phone, especially when she was trying to talk to him. Jacob had felt like he was merely multitasking, listening to her while also responding to texts. To Olivia, this felt like an insult. Was he really listening, and why didn't he care enough to give her his full attention? Jacob learned the discipline of setting his phone down to listen to Olivia.

If I invest thirty minutes in a quality conversation with you, then I have essentially given you thirty minutes of my life. That undivided, focused attention communicates that I care, that you matter to me— and this is especially true if your primary love language is Time.

Talking

In addition to active listening, quality conversation also involves talking, of course. Some people have not yet developed the communication skills necessary for quality conversation.

Like Savannah. Her relationships never lasted. Guys found her entertaining at first, but they didn't really connect with her. One guy told her he just didn't feel like he knew her. She thought about that a lot and finally realized that even though she talked a lot, she didn't really say anything about herself. In her house there was constant noise and no depth. Safe topics were the weather, sports, and the price of a dozen apples at the Produce Junction, but zero self-revelation.

Dylan's problem manifested itself differently. Like Savannah, he struggled to connect deeply with others, but that's because he said almost nothing. The irony is that Dylan had an incredible sense of humor. He was witty and had a quick answer to everything—in his head. In Dylan's home, his older sisters dominated every conversation, so he never developed his verbal skills.

There's hope for people like Savannah and Dylan. It begins with realizing the need to open up; then learning to tap into emotions, thoughts, and desires; and then becoming comfortable verbalizing those things. It's the process of resocializing: going back and replacing the dysfunctional patterns of childhood with healthy patterns of communication. It's not easy, but it is necessary in order to speak the dialect of quality conversation. People like Dylan may never become avid conversationalists or eloquent public speakers, but with those closest to them, they can learn to feel comfortable and let loose with humor. People like Savannah may still talk about the weather with strangers, but within close relationships, they can learn to reveal enough about themselves to really connect. For all of us, there's hope.

DIALECT #2: QUALITY LISTENING

Some people are rotten listeners. They listen just long enough to get the topic of the conversation and then proceed to tell you all their stories tied to that topic. Give them any conversation thread, and within minutes, they can spin that conversation so it's all about them. How much do you enjoy talking to self-centered people like that?

And then there are the fix-it people. If you start to describe a personal struggle, these friends give you a tidy solution. They're skilled at analyzing problems and proposing solutions but not at sympathetic listening.

"I ALWAYS THOUGHT I WAS HELPING PEOPLE BY GIVING THEM ADVICE. OVER TIME I REALIZED THAT JUST COMES ACROSS AS BOSSY. OR CONTROLLING. I DON'T WANT TO BE THAT GUY, SO NOW I DON'T OFFER ADVICE UNLESS SOMEONE ASKS, AND THEN ONLY SPARINGLY. NOW PEOPLE FEEL MORE COMFORTABLE TALKING TO ME."

—ETHAN

The goal of quality listening is *understanding*. Kate has learned to preface some of what she says to her boyfriend with the following words: "I just need you to hear me. I don't need you to fix this." These words detour around frustration, and she gives him a clear clue about what she needs: to be heard.

Sympathetic Listening Skills

Want to hone your skills as a listener? Try these practical ideas.

1. *Maintain eye contact.* This keeps your mind from wandering and communicates that the person has your full attention. No eye rolling, staring vacantly into space, or people watching.

2. *Avoid multitasking.* No listening + texting + driving + cooking + finishing your essay. Remember, Quality Time involves giving someone your undivided attention. If you're in the middle of something, tell it like it is rather than faking it. "I'm interested in what you're saying, but I'm super focused on _____ right now and can't give you my full attention. Can we pause this conversation for ten minutes?" That's a far more elegant approach than half-listening.

3. *Listen for feelings.* Listen not just for events but also for emotions. When you think you're tracking, confirm it: "It sounds like you are feeling disappointed because of _____" or "I hear your anger." This gives the speaker the chance to clarify his feelings and confirms that you're listening intently to what's being said.

4. *Observe body language.* Some researchers claim communication is 93 percent nonverbal and only 7 percent verbal. Others slice that number differently, but the consensus is this: *content* is dwarfed by *tone*. As you read the other person's body language, again ask for clarification: "You said you miss him, but you look mad. Do you have mixed feelings?"

5. *Don't interrupt.* If you interrupt someone to interject your own ideas, you derail her train of thought, and she may never reach her destination. Even if you feel like you need to defend yourself or set

the other person straight, zip it. Your goal? *To understand,* not to be right or to give advice.

6. *Ask reflective questions.* When you think you understand what the person is saying, check it out by reflecting back what you're hearing, like this: "What I hear you saying is _____. Is that correct?" Reflective listening allows you to confirm or correct your perception of the person's message.

7. *Express empathy.* The speaker needs to know that you *get* it.

Let's say Noah is venting to Rachel about their yearbook sponsor. As one of the editors this year, Noah is investing a ton of his free time in yearbook, in addition to the yearbook class period every day.

By empathizing, Rachel is affirming Noah's sense of worth and legitimizing his feelings.

8. *Ask if there's anything you can do to help.* Key distinction: offer your services rather than tell the person what to do. Noah doesn't want advice. He just needs his friend to be supportive when he vents. If he's stumped and asks for advice, then Rachel could

share ideas. No unsolicited advice!

Quality conversations take time and thought. In fact, you'll spend twice as much time listening as talking. The payoff, though, is enormous. By listening well, you make the other person feel respected, understood, and loved—which is the goal of quality conversation.

DIALECT #3: QUALITY ACTIVITIES

The love language of Time has a third dialect: quality activities. **The emphasis is on being together, doing an activity together, and giving each other undivided attention.**

At a 5LL event, I asked participants to complete the following prompt: "I feel most loved by _____ when _____." They could insert the name of anyone: parent, friend, boyfriend/girlfriend. This was Tyler's response:

> *"I FEEL MOST LOVED BY MY DAD WHEN WE DO THINGS TOGETHER. LIKE GO TO A HOCKEY GAME OR KAYAK OR HIKE. I DON'T CARE IF HE BUYS ME A BIG CHRISTMAS PRESENT OR WRITES ME A BIRTHDAY CARD OR ANYTHING. IT'S REALLY JUST ABOUT BEING TOGETHER."*

Tyler's response reveals that his primary love language is Time, and his natural dialect is quality activities.

Quality activities may include anything in which one or both of you has an interest. The emphasis is not on *what* you are doing but on *why* you are doing it—to experience something together.

Entering into another person's interests may stretch you. For the sake of someone you love, you might go to your first country music concert, car race, book club, NFL game, cooking class, or art show. The other person walks away feeling loved. *He cares about me enough to try something I enjoy, and he did it with an open mind.* That is love, and for some people, it is love's loudest voice.

Such intentional quality activities take some planning—and sacrifice. It might mean trying something you don't particularly enjoy (like the girl who hates being cold but tries downhill skiing to be with her brothers). But by spending time together and entering into another's world, you learn to speak the love language of Time.

One of the cool by-products of quality activities is shared memories. *Remember the 4,400-mile road trip? Remember that camping trip when we both got poison ivy? Remember that night game at Wrigley Field? Remember the new ride at Six Flags? Remember the concert in the rain? Remember hiking Camelback on the hottest day of the summer? Remember that day we got lost in the city? Remember that rickety beach house your family rented? Remember when that dog chased us when we were training for the 5K?*

Those are memories of love, especially for the person whose primary love language is Time and whose native dialect is quality activities.

// WARNING: BE INCLUSIVE // Every love language has an opposite. The opposite of giving someone your time is intentionally, deliberately leaving someone out. We see this cruelty enacted every day—in the classroom, at lunch, on the social scene, in any group setting. And we all know how it feels to be left out—that lonely, pit-in-your-stomach, sad feeling.

Children are overtly cruel. In the lunchroom: "No, you can't sit here. I'm saving that seat for my friend." Ouch. On the playground: "No, you can't play with us. Only four players." Ouch.

But older students and adults can be just as cruel; we only mask it more subtly. We "forget" to include someone, or make eye contact with everyone in the conversation except one person, or form a study group that's "full," or talk openly about a party that one person wasn't invited to, or start practicing together in a closed group, or . . . The list is endless. No doubt you could fill in more scenarios or cruel behaviors you've witnessed, experienced, or even enacted yourself. Think *Mean Girls*.

Everyone wants to feel included, especially Quality Time people. That wound of being left out hurts them extra deeply. Whenever we have the opportunity, we should be kind to others and make them feel included.

Can you invite everyone you know to your party? It depends on the type of party (and your parents), but you'll likely have to limit the invitations. You don't have to advertise it, though, or talk openly about the party in front of those who weren't included, or post pictures of it to show what an amazing time it was for those lucky enough to be invited.

Can everyone who tries out for the volleyball team make it? No. The coach can't carry the entire school on the team roster. And while there's a certain bond within the tribe—the privilege of belonging—you don't have to flaunt it in front of others. Outside volleyball settings, you can change the conversation topic so everyone can participate.

Can you sit with every single friend and acquaintance at lunch or in a class? Not possible. But you can go out of your way to be kind and inclusive. "There's another seat over here," or "Save me a spot tomorrow," or "I have a funny story to tell you—I'll find you after lunch."

Students who master these social dynamics of being kind and inclusive tend to have a lot of friends. People are drawn to them.

Want to become a better friend? For some people this is so natural and instinctive. For others, it's helpful to break down the technique:

1. Invite/include someone. ("Lunch today?")
2. Ask for his or her input. ("Chipotle or Subway?")

3. Ask personal questions about the person's life. ("What was your old school like?")

4. Listen well. (Shhh, you're listening. Silence is golden.)

This works with everyone, not just Time people. The difference is that Time people will feel especially loved and valued by being included, while others just really, really like it. Being inclusive is a great way to make and keep friends.

TOO BUSY FOR EACH OTHER

Each person who draws breath on this earth receives the same amount of time each day: 24 hours, 1,440 minutes, or 86,400 seconds.

At the end of that day, the time is gone.

Time cannot be stolen, exchanged, refunded, stockpiled, or hacked. Time is extremely limited—yet insanely in demand. Think of all that competes for your time: school, homework, work, working out, drama, clubs, sports, music, church, family, friends, dating, volunteering, hobbies, sleep, relaxation.

How will you spend your time?

Many of us live at a frantic pace. Our calendars are overflowing. We run from one activity to the next. There's constant noise in our lives. We're always connected. But are we actually connecting with others?

The love language of Quality Time requires *time*. That seems so simple, but is it?

There's the parent who's often gone on business trips and not always available for his or her family.

Then there's the parent who is so overwhelmed and worn down from trying to keep up with all the kids' activities, when really, all the kids want is for someone to just sit still and listen to them for five minutes.

Then there's the little brother who's starved for attention, who just wants someone to see and hear him and treat him like he's important too.

Then there's the friend whose siblings are so high maintenance that she gets completely overlooked.

And then there's you. Will you get seduced by the idea that busyness equals importance? Or can you *make* time to spend with those you love?

Love is a choice. Love is a verb.

PAUSE & PROCESS

1. Remember, of the five love languages, most people have one favorite. Is Time your primary love language—does it make you feel especially good or loved?
2. Are you energized when you spend quality time with others, or does it tend to deplete you emotionally?
3. To what degree is the love language of Time spoken by members of your family?
4. With whom have you spent quality time this week? Was your time together primarily quality conversation or activities?
5. Would you describe yourself as an inclusive person? If not, is this an area of growth for you? How can you consciously be kinder and more inclusive in your social settings this week?
6. What kind of a listener are you? What practical ideas from this chapter would help you become a better listener?
7. Review your list of primary relationships, that handful of people closest to you. Is Time the love language of one of your people?
8. Entering into others' interests takes planning. Brainstorm a new activity to try together. Be creative! And be intentional—get it on the schedule in advance.

CHAPTER 3

LOVE LANGUAGE #3: GIFTS

What is your most prized possession? Maybe you've run through this scenario in your mind: "If the house catches on fire, and I only have time to grab one thing, what would I rescue?" (Disclaimers: Everyone got out safely, including your dog, and your item of choice was within reach. Of course you didn't foolishly run back into the flames! And the insurance policy on your house was comprehensive and up-to-date, so stop hyperventilating. Okay, back to the story.)

What did you pick? Was it the most valuable item you own, in strictly monetary terms? Your iPad, your designer jeans, your entire collection of Xbox games? Probably not. You likely chose something of sentimental value to you. **And therein lies the first lesson about Gifts—the value of an item isn't in its price tag but in its meaning to the person.**

Virtually everyone has a profound story that relates to the love language known as Gifts. Gifts are more than material items; they become positive or negative symbols. On the positive side, they can represent appreciation, value, sacrifice, love, devotion, loyalty, or celebration. On the negative side, they can represent guilt, bribery, failure, thoughtlessness, fear, or cruelty. Gifts are always received as an extension of the giver.

gifts: *noun* 1. MORE THAN A MATERIAL ITEM 2. A VISUAL SYMBOL OF LOVE 3. REPRESENTING THE GIVER

THE MEANING OF A GIFT

A gift is a tangible object that communicates "I was thinking about you. I wanted you to have this. I love you."

This is universal and timeless. Anthropologists have never discovered a culture in which gift giving is not an expression of love. Giving gifts is one of the fundamental languages of love.

Some gifts only last for a few hours. Remember picking a dandelion (or your neighbor's tulips) to give to your mom? The gift quickly wilted, but the memory has undoubtedly stayed with your mom for years. Other gifts endure for a lifetime, even outlasting the giver—your grandmother's simple gold wedding band or your grandfather's type from his printing press. What's priceless is not the gift itself but the emotional love that was communicated by the gift. The right gift is any token, big or small, that conveys the giver's love.

Our English word *gift* is derived from the Greek word *charis,* which means "grace" or "an undeserved gift." By its very nature, a gift is not payment for services rendered. When someone offers, "I will give you _____ if you will _____," this person is striking a deal, not offering a gift. A gift has no strings attached—if it does, it ceases to be a gift.

Nor is a gift a substitute for an apology or restitution. You can't cheat on your girlfriend and then buy her flowers. Roses don't cover a multitude of sins. You can't scream at your brother and then buy him a Frappuccino to make it up to him. You can't break curfew but unload the dishwasher and expect your relationship with your mom to be kosher. A gift is a gift only when given as a genuine expression of love, not as an effort to cover over past failures.

A gift is a visual symbol of love. The gift can be any size, shape, color, or price. It may be purchased, found, or made. To the individual whose primary love language is Gifts, the cost of the gift doesn't matter. You can purchase a designer card or make a homemade card from recycled paper—as long as it reflects your thought and the recipient's taste, then it's meaningful.

LEARNING THE LANGUAGE OF GIFTS

This may not come naturally to you at first. You might worry, "I'm not a good gift giver. I have no idea how to select gifts." Fear not, and congratulations! You have just made a fundamental discovery about loving people: it takes work. Love often requires learning a language you have never spoken. Fortunately, gift giving is one of the easiest love languages to learn.

Like all love languages, the more specific and personal you speak it, the more loved the recipient feels. What most people with the love language of Gifts want others to understand is that they value being known. **They feel loved because someone took the time and effort to get them something personal and thoughtful.** Excellent gift giving is only accomplished by getting to know someone well, which requires a detective mindset.

Two tips to help you perfect the art of gift giving: *First, listen closely.* Your friend might be talking about her new favorite author. Why not buy her another book by that writer? Your sister might always borrow her friend's gray hoodie. Check out the brand and size, and buy one for her. Your mom might have lost her favorite headphones. An easy gift idea. Your dad might complain that he shanked his last Titleist Pro V1 golf ball in the pond. Why not buy him a sleeve for Father's Day? Your friend becomes a rabid Barcelona fan. How about a Barcelona T-shirt or jersey for his birthday? Everyday life yields lots of clues about the people you love so you can find the perfect gift to match the recipient. Just listen.

Second, make a list. Otherwise, the next birthday rolls around and you draw a big, fat blank. Try keeping a note on your phone: "Gift ideas for Matthew." Or put items in your Amazon cart to "save for later." Wait till you see the reaction to this level of thoughtful gift giving: "I can't believe you remembered how much I like this!" Or "I only mentioned this once, like six months ago."

Back in the day, the perfect gift was the old-school mixtape. On a mixtape, you could choppily record all your favorite songs from the radio or copy songs from your other tapes and create a personalized mixtape for someone. It took a lot of time, the result was pretty scratchy, but it sure showed care. The gift was technically inexpensive but thoughtful and valuable.

Gifts like the mixtape show that you were thinking of someone. "Gift This Song" on iTunes. Create a playlist. Forward the funny link about the cat yoga class. Order the frumpy $5 cross-stitch pillow set that you know will make your friend laugh. Frame a favorite photo, or create a photo book from your vacation together. Pick up fresh flowers or peaches from a farmer's market. Register a star in someone's name. Hide a gift in a packed suitcase. Little, thoughtful gestures can be valuable gifts that show you care.

THE COLLECTION

If someone you love really enjoys gifts, then look for the easy, ongoing gift idea: *the collection.* Does the person already have a collection in process? Then be on the lookout for missing items. Or can you start a new collection for someone? Then think of what that person would find interesting:

- Rare baseball cards
- Christmas ornaments
- Quarters from each of the fifty states
- Vintage art or books
- Funky coffee mugs
- Pokémon cards (for a younger sibling)
- Silver charm bracelet

For example, if your mom loves jewelry, then a charm bracelet might be a perfect gift for her. The initial outlay for the bracelet may seem a little steep, but this is an investment. The charms, which are relatively inexpensive, are what make this an ideal gift. You can personalize the bracelet by finding charms that she'd love: her initials, her favorite gem, favorite vacation spot, favorite animal, a heart, "mom," and so on. Over time, the charm bracelet becomes distinctly hers, with each charm a memory of your relationship with her.

$$$

We all come from different financial backgrounds that color our attitudes about spending money. If you have a spending orientation, then you'll likely feel good about spending money on gifts. If you have a saving perspective, then saving money feels good while spending might pain you. You might think, *I don't buy much for myself. Why would I lavish cash on others?*

To improve as a giver, you may have to adjust your attitude about money. Big spenders may have to discover the value of free or inexpensive gifts. Aggressive savers may have to shift their perspective and see that spending a little money may be a wise investment. Buying gifts for those you love invests in your relationships and fills others' love tanks.

Avoid the financial extremes: You'll never want to go into credit card debt to become the world's most generous gift giver. Nor do you want to morph into stingy, old Scrooge who can't part with his money. Working within your means, you can be both wise and generous.

Just like the old-school mixtape, a thoughtful gift can be pretty inexpensive.

THE GIFT OF PRESENCE

There's one dialect of gift giving that is intangible but highly important: the gift of self, or the gift of presence. Physically being there when your loved one needs you speaks loudly to the person whose primary love language is Gifts.

Don't underestimate the tremendous power of presence. Physical presence in the time of crisis is the most powerful gift you can give; not only are you physically there, but your being present is a symbol of your love. Remove the symbol, and the sense of love evaporates.

For the Gifts person in your life—when crisis strikes, show up.

// WARNING: SKIP THE BRIBERY // Every love language has an opposite. The opposite of sincere, thoughtful gift giving is bribery–giving a gift in order to get something in return or to unduly influence someone. Bribery always involves a false, ulterior motive. At first the giver might not ask you to do or give anything in return, but eventually the person will. If you refuse, then the giver may try to manipulate or guilt you. Bribery comes in many flavors and colors: the student who tries to buy your friendship, the friend who doesn't want you to tell on her, the stranger or acquaintance who offers you something so you will go somewhere with him. Be suspicious and savvy. Look past the shiny gift to the giver's motivation.

Bribery Survival Strategies

1. Politely refuse the gift. "No thanks." This short-circuits the bribe entirely.

2. Talk with someone wise (a parent, teacher, coach, mentor, older sibling) to get a second opinion. "How would you interpret this?"

3. Don't let yourself get into an isolated situation. When you were a little kid, the lesson was not to climb into a car with a stranger. For teens and adults, the lesson is not to get lured away from the crowd by someone you don't know. When in doubt, evacuate.

4. Trust your gut. If your instincts tell you something is off and you just don't feel comfortable, don't ignore that sixth sense. There's a reason God gave you hairs on the back of your neck.

RECOGNIZING GIFTS AS SOMEONE'S PRIMARY LANGUAGE

For some people, Gifts is their primary love language. Gifts make them feel loved most deeply, though they might feel hesitant to talk about it, fearing it makes them seem selfish. But this isn't about materialism; it's about the symbolic value of a well-chosen gift. Once you discover that someone's love language is Gifts, you should intentionally give him or her more gifts than you would another person.

Sometimes people mistakenly assume that Gifts people will only like a gift if it's expensive. False. Remember, they see a gift as an extension of the giver, so more important than dollar value is sincerity. That's not to say they don't like expensive gifts! They like virtually all gifts that are given in the right way.

When Ben started dating Hannah, it didn't take long for him to figure out she valued gifts. The first time she invited him to come over, she told him the story behind every little object on the family room bookshelf. What looked to Ben like clutter was pure treasure for Hannah.

In order to make Hannah feel loved, Ben will never miss a

birthday or special occasion, and he will also find random excuses to give her little gifts: the first day of summer break, happy six-month anniversary, last snow day of junior year. When Ben travels, he'll do more than just send Hannah a postcard ("Greetings from Sunny San Diego"); he'll give her the eye-catching stone from the mountain trail he hiked, the home run ball he caught at a game, or a specialty chocolate bar from the pier. These surprise gifts will express his love and mean a lot to Hannah. She will know that even when Ben is away from her, he's thinking about her.

This doesn't mean you speak only the primary love language of the people you care for. Love can and should be expressed and received in all five languages. However, if you don't speak a person's primary love language, then that person will not feel loved, even though you may be fluently speaking the other four. Once you speak their primary love language, then the person can hear your love loudly in all five.

And even if you know someone's love language isn't Gifts, that doesn't exempt you on birthdays and holidays. It would be rude to brush off your mom on Mother's Day. Even if Gifts isn't her primary love language, she will still really like that present you picked out for her.

PAUSE & PROCESS

1. Remember, of the five love languages, most people have one favorite. Is Gifts your primary love language—do gifts make you feel especially good or loved?
2. What is the most meaningful gift you've ever received and why?
3. To what degree is the love language of Gifts spoken by members of your family?
4. From the imaginary scenario at the beginning of the chapter, which item would you theoretically grab from your burning house? Why is this item so valuable to you?
5. If you could receive any gift in the world, what would you choose and why?
6. Advertisements can twist the meaning of gifts. Analyze commercials you see. How do jewelry commercials, for example, imply that every recipient is exactly the same? How do commercials falsely correlate the price of a gift with the givers' love?
7. How can the love language of Gifts become warped in both modest and well-off families? If a kid whose love language is Gifts grows up in a family struggling to get by, how can that family overcome financial challenges and still communicate love? On the other extreme, in a family with seemingly unlimited wealth, how can an abundance of gifts create the suspicion that none of them actually represents love? How can that family better communicate love?
8. Interview your closest people. Ask them about their favorite gifts and what those items mean to them. This will give you clues about whose primary love language is Gifts.

CHAPTER 4

LOVE LANGUAGE #4: SERVICE

Mackenzie heard the garage door open and rushed to hide the last of the evidence. She dashed to the laundry room with the broom, paper towels, rags, and spray cleaner and quickly put them away. By the time her mom walked up the stairs, Mackenzie was lounging on her bed, looking idly at her phone.

"How was your day, Mac?" her mom asked, her voice sounding thin and tired. Mac looked up at her mom and managed to keep a straight face. "Good except for gym class. Badminton *again*," she said with a comical pout.

Her mom cracked a small smile and walked off to change.

Three minutes later, she came back to Mac's room, beaming, full of joy and energy. "Oh Mac, you cleaned the bathroom for me! You know I hate that job, and I was dreading it this weekend. Thank you!" Not that Mac loves spraying Windex either—but her mom's expression made that frenzied half hour of cleaning totally worth it.

Mac's not a professional house cleaner. She's more of a linguist, since she can speak her mom's native love language—Acts of Service. Mac had been watching her mom navigate a busy week at work and home, and she knew the one thing that would make her mom feel most loved was to get her hands dirty (literally) by cleaning the bathroom for her. Because Mac loves her mom, she cleaned. **Remember, love is an action.** This becomes abundantly clear in the love language of Service.

service: *noun* 1. DOING SOMETHING KIND 2. INTENTIONAL 3. UNEXPECTED 4. THAT HELPS SOMEONE ELSE

UNEXPECTED

The sticking point in the definition of Service is the adjective "unexpected." If you get an allowance every week for a set regimen of chores (making your bed, taking out the trash, feeding your crazy old cat, etc.), then taking out the trash doesn't qualify as an act of service. You're expected to do that; it's part of the social contract for living in your home. Cleaning up your room doesn't qualify as service either. If you live like a slovenly pig, then you should be expected to pick up the mountain of clothes piled in the middle of your bedroom floor.

Service goes beyond the expected into the realm of the unexpected—like how Mac cleaned the bathroom. She intentionally did something kind, surprised her mom, and relieved her mom's workload. That's service.

IMPACT

When it comes to communicating love through service, you can't just *try harder*. **You have to consider which acts of service will have the most *impact* on the recipient.**

- You could spend eight hours weeding the forest at your grandparents' lake house, getting 376 mosquito bites in the process, or you could spend four minutes making your bed so your grandma doesn't gag every time she walks past your bedroom. Which has more impact?

- You could alphabetize your dad's entire library, your hands covered in paper-cut wounds, or you could simply fill his car up with gas so the next time he needs to go somewhere, he won't regret letting you borrow it. Which has more impact?
- You could match every one of your little brother's disgusting socks so he has actual pairs in his drawer, or you could spend two minutes gluing the head back on his decapitated dinosaur, as he'd begged you to do. Which has more impact?
- You could drive three hours to a farmer's market to buy fresh avocados, your girlfriend's favorite food, or you could show up with a new pack of printer paper, since she ran out while working on her stressful research paper that's due tomorrow. Which has more impact?

When it comes to Acts of Service, you're not judged by the amount of time you put in or even by how hard you work. You're judged by your effectiveness—the impact you make on the person you love.

Think of it this way. A starting pitcher in baseball may work on his delivery constantly, making sure the release point of his off-speed pitches matches that of his fastball. He may take hundreds of extra ground balls and line drives after practice in a quest to field his position better. He may study hours of film every week, learning the tendencies of various batters.

In the end, though, he's judged by one criterion: does he get people out? If the answer is no, then it doesn't matter how long or hard he worked in practice. What matters is the impact he has in the game.

This lesson applies in service. We don't show love by doing every little slave task available each day. That's working too hard—at the wrong tasks. **To fill the love tanks of our people, we have to serve** selectively, considering what will have the most *impact*, taking the *initiative* to serve in the way that will be meaningful to the other, and serving with the right *attitude*.

True service involves . . .

your hands: Let's state the obvious. You have to actually *do* something.

your heart: The motivation for service is love—not bartering, manipulation, or showing off. Just love.

your brain: Think hard to choose a meaningful act. Rearranging your mom's kitchen? Bad idea. Emptying the dishwasher for your mom? Brilliant move.

INITIATIVE

Morgan used to love to give blood. It felt so noble, picturing her blood helping to save the life of a survivor of a car accident or someone undergoing surgery. With admittedly a little swell of pride, she liked walking out of the blood bank with her sticker on her shirt: "I GAVE BLOOD TODAY." She was a true believer, even an evangelist, recruiting others to give blood too.

Then one day she was rejected. During the registration process, donors fill out reams of paperwork and then get screened. That day she discovered her iron deficiency. "Sorry," Morgan was told, "maybe next time." They still gave her a sticker, but this one read, "I BELIEVE IN GIVING BLOOD."

There's a difference between *giving* blood and *believing* in giving blood, and that day, Morgan felt the sour, humiliating difference.

Everyone else walked out with their real stickers and Band-Aids, and she walked out with what she felt was a sad excuse for a sticker. Let's apply that concept to Service. Do you *serve*, or do you *believe* in serving?

After practice, do you cheerfully say goodbye and then watch your coach struggle singlehandedly to collect all the balls, pinnies, and cones and schlep them to his car like a pack mule? Or without saying a word, do you help?

At home, when you watch your dad return from an exhausting day at work to rake leaves or mow the lawn, do you wave to him from the couch, or do you pick up a rake?

At school, do you watch your technology-challenged friend struggling to upload his assignment and blithely wander away? Or do you quietly sit down next to him and patiently teach him how to do it (even if it's the ninth time)?

After your mom cooks a gourmet dinner, do you run out to meet your friends, or do you text them you'll be late and then stay to help her clean up?

When you find out that your lonely grandpa needs a ride to his doctor appointment, do you avoid eye contact, hoping you can make plans with friends that day, or do you volunteer to drive him?

Do you *serve*—or do you *believe* in serving?

There's also a difference between choosing to serve and being coerced into service. That difference is initiative. When you take initiative, you see a need, and you choose to meet that need without even being asked. If your parents write out a list of chores that need to be done before the family party next weekend, you can (A) wait until they nag you seventeen times before stirring from your self-involved stupor, or (B) take some initiative, scan the list, pick something you can do well, and do it. Either way, you may have to clean the basement; but in scenario A, your parents are ready to auction you off on eBay, and in scenario B, your parents brag about you at the party. It's your choice, and it comes down to initiative.

Remember, every time you delay or refuse to serve, you send a clear message: *this task isn't important to me.* It's hard for someone not to take that personally and assume you mean something more: *you aren't important to me.*

Love is always freely given. It can't be demanded, cajoled, or coaxed from someone. That's why it's vital that you take the *initiative* in completing acts of service for those you love. Otherwise, it doesn't feel like love.

ATTITUDE

Just as crucial as the actual act of service itself is the *attitude* with which you perform it. In fact, the right thing done with the wrong attitude can actually cause more harm than good. If your mom senses resentment or irritation in you while you're performing an act of service for her, then she won't feel affirmed. She'll feel irritated and start counting down the days till you go off to college. If you treat her like an imposition, a bother, a drain on your time and energy, where's the love in that?

For maximum *impact,* your acts of service should be done with eagerness—an excitement to do something meaningful for someone you love. They should be done with good humor (even the tasks you routinely hate). And they should be done with humility. Don't call attention to yourself while you're performing them. Don't make a big deal about them afterward. Refuse to play the hero card or the martyr card. Remember who you're doing them for and why.

// WARNING: THE DOORMAT SYNDROME // Service ≠ slavery.
Remember that symbol from math class? Service does not equal slavery.

Big difference. Slavery is at the heart of dysfunctional families. When people
serve others because they are forced to do so, freedom to truly serve is lost.
Slavery hardens the heart and creates anger, bitterness, and resentment.

Imagine this (all-too-real) scenario. If a wife serves her husband tirelessly for
years, waiting on him hand and foot, while he takes her for granted, ignores her,
and humiliates her in front of his friends, how will she feel?

Or here's another (all-too-real) scenario. Picture two friends: one the queen
bee, the other a wannabe. If the second girl does everything the first wants,
hoping to become more popular or be closer friends, while the first girl takes her
for granted, ignores her, and uses her, how will the weaker girl feel?

Like a doormat. You wipe your feet on it and step all over it. The doormat has
no will of its own. When you treat another person as an object, you preclude the
possibility of real love. Manipulation is not the language of love: "If you love me,
then you will do this for me." Coercion by fear has no place in love: "You will do
this for me, or you will be sorry."

You should never treat someone like a doormat. Not your parent. Not your
sibling. Not your friend. Not the person you're dating.

Nor should you ever let yourself be treated like a doormat. **Allowing yourself to be used or mistreated by another person isn't actually loving.** It
is, in fact, an act of treason. Doormat mode allows the manipulator to develop
inhumane habits. Love says, "I love myself enough to demand better treatment,
and I love you too much to let you treat me this way. It's not good for you or
me." Love is strong.

In healthy relationships, true love often finds its expression in acts of service—
service freely given, not out of fear or because of abuse, but by choice. Those
who love, serve; and those who serve discover the truth that "it is more blessed
to give than to receive." [3]

THE MODEL

Want to know what service looks like? Take a look at the Master. It was the very last night of Jesus' life on earth. He knew what was coming: betrayal, trial, torture, and death. He spent His last evening with the disciples.

Now if you knew you were on death row, wouldn't you treat your last few hours as if they were all about you? You might invite your friends over to keep you company, ask your mom to make your favorite meal, make your siblings do your every whim so you could relax and face death with dignity.

Not Jesus. Knowing it was His last night, He spent it serving His disciples. "Having loved his own who were in the world, he loved them to the end."[4] Jesus showed them love by a dramatic act of service. Mid-dinner, Jesus stood up, wrapped a towel around His waist, took a basin of water, and washed each disciple's feet.

What a repulsive job. Back in the day, people wore open sandals, walked on dusty roads (shared by animals), and bathed infrequently. Their feet were caked with sweat and dirt. Gross. Jesus—their Teacher and Lord—was the One who got low and served.

He washed all twenty-four feet. Even Judas's. Even though Jesus knew Judas was about to betray Him. And when He finished, He asked them, "Do you understand what I have done for you?" Blank stares from the disciples, still in shock over the foot-washing. "Now that I, your Lord and Teacher, have washed your feet, you also should wash one another's feet. I have set you an example that you should do as I have done for you."[5]

Get it? Love serves.

GRATITUDE

Little kids expect to be served. They aren't expected to earn a living, pay the property taxes, cook dinner, or even get themselves to school on time. Their parents manage all of that. That's natural.

The maturity shift happens when older kids receive their parents' benefits without taking them for granted. It's an attitude shift from "I deserve" to "I'm thankful."

Serving others makes a difference in many lives—especially your own. **Doing acts of service for others opens your eyes to all that others do for you.** For example, cleaning the bathroom one time reminds you that your mom did it the other fifty-one times. Service is an equalizer, changing the relationship from one-way receiving to two-way giving and receiving. Those who serve tend to be far more grateful than those who simply receive.

The Service Revolution

Need some extra ideas to spark your own service revolution?

1. Make breakfast for your mom on her birthday.
2. Carry the groceries in from the car.
3. Do your brother's chores during his finals week.
4. Water the flowers at a neighbor's house without getting paid.
5. Ask your teacher, "Need any help?"
6. Volunteer for Habitat for Humanity.
7. Teach the wild, little preschoolers at church.
8. Write down homework assignments for an absent friend.
9. Serve as a family at the homeless shelter.
10. Visit your friend whose dad has cancer (and take cinnamon rolls).
11. Help your dyslexic friend organize her personal narrative.
12. Vacuum the upstairs carpet.

PAUSE & PROCESS

1. Remember, of the five love languages, most people have one favorite. Is Service your primary love language—do acts of service make you feel especially good or loved?

2. Think of a memorable time someone served you. What makes that act of service stand out in your mind?

3. To what degree is the love language of Service spoken by members of your family?

4. How freely do you express acts of service to others? What holds you back?

5. What acts of service have you done for members of your family in the last month?

6. What acts of service have you shown toward a friend or someone you're dating?

7. What acts of service have others done for you lately?

8. Review your list of important relationships. (This should be a handful of relationships, not a boatload.) Pick an act of service that would be meaningful to each of those people, and then notice how each responds to being served. If you get a low-key "Oh, thanks," then Service isn't that person's primary love language. If your act of service means the world to the person, then *lightbulb!* You just discovered someone's primary love language.

CHAPTER 5

LOVE LANGUAGE #5: TOUCH

In the runaway bestselling book *Wonder* by R. J. Palacio, the main character, August, has a severe facial deformity. August experiences a rough transition from being homeschooled to attending fifth grade at Beecher Prep, his first time going off to school. Auggie realizes, "I noticed not too long ago that even though people were getting used to me, no one would actually touch me. I didn't realize this at first because it's not like kids go around touching each other that much in middle school anyway."

But then August starts to notice some more obvious clues—a girl having a panic attack when partnered with him in gym class; lab partners fighting to sit on the opposite side of the table; students treating August like he's a monster. In fact, the kids at Beecher Prep invent something called the Plague: "Anyone who accidentally touches August has only thirty seconds to wash their hands or find hand sanitizer before they catch the Plague."[6] How the students withhold touch from Auggie is outright cruel. They treat him like a diseased outcast.

How would you feel if everyone refused to touch you?

Human beings have trillions of nerve cells. From birth, we cry out for physical touch. Studies show that infants who are not touched are more likely to be physically, mentally, and emotionally delayed. In extreme cases, babies who received minimal touch have actually died. Babies inherently understand their need for touch, which explains why they will often stop crying when they're picked up. Tender, affirming Touch is a fundamental language of love.

That's true for all of us. What's tricky is that in some stages of life, we don't get touched that much. Strangers pet dogs and feel free to touch babies or even rub pregnant women's bellies (which is just weird). But sometimes even the most loving dad can get all awkward around his teenage son or daughter. The same dad who used to throw you on his shoulders might act distant around you now. He doesn't know how he's supposed to relate to you. The result can be loneliness and physical isolation.

The body is designed for touch. Of the five senses, touch is unlike the others in that it's not limited to one localized area of the body. Tiny tactile receptors are located throughout the whole body. When those receptors are pressed, nerves carry impulses to the brain, the brain interprets these impulses, and we perceive and translate the touch: warm or cold, harsh or gentle, painful or pleasurable, loving or hostile.

physical touch: *adjective +* *noun* **1.** INTENTIONAL **2.** MEANINGFUL **3.** HUMAN CONTACT **4.** TO MAKE THE RECIPIENT FEEL LOVED

Physical touch can make or break a relationship. It can communicate hate or love. If someone's primary love language is Touch, then your touches speak more loudly than your words. If you withhold touch, the person will feel isolated and doubt your love. If a friend feels low and you clasp his shoulder, you're communicating,

"I care. You're not alone." Touch communicates emotionally, not just physically.

THE BUBBLE-WRAP FAMILY

Some families are very physical. You can't walk through their house without getting hugged, kissed, wrestled, or shoved. In their home, touch is normal.

Some families aren't too into touch. They only hug each other at funerals or kiss their kids as they leave for a twelve-week summer camp. This isn't bad; it's just factual. This only becomes problematic if your love language happens to be Touch and you come from a family that would prefer to wear bubble-wrap suits. In these situations, you may need to go on the offensive—grab your mom and dad in a hug, and train them to hug you back. Once parents realize their kids need Touch, they can usually deliver.

THE GENDER GAP

Have you ever noticed the gender gap in physical touch? Girls touch each other, and guys touch each other, but it looks different.

Imagine two girls, close friends, greeting each other first thing in the morning at school. They might hug as if they haven't seen each other in ages. Normal.

Imagine two guys, close friends, greeting each other first thing in the morning at school. They might do "the man hug," where they grab hands like they're going to arm wrestle and then move quickly toward each other and back. You couldn't really call it a "hug." It looks more like a gang greeting. Also normal.

Boys and girls tend to express touch very differently as they get older. While you might see girls sit close together or do each other's hair, most guys sit farther apart and prefer to wrestle (and they don't do each other's hair, unless you count dumping a water bottle over a friend's head). Both genders get their touch, but it looks differ-ent. Boys tend to love contact sports, such as football, hockey, and wrestling. They tackle their teammates to celebrate in the end zone, and they even wrestle each other down the hallway. They engage in touch, and it's not gentle. Touch is socially conditioned by gender.

Touch is also constrained by expectations of age. Kids comfort-ably, naturally, fluidly touch each other. Arm wrestling. Thumb wres-tling. Tag at recess. Bloody knuckles. Marco Polo in the pool. Left to their own devices, kids (especially boys) can make a contact sport out of any game or activity, even reading. And then we're expected to outgrow that. As we grow older, we keep our distance. Adult inter-actions are mostly contact-free, aside from the occasional hand-shake or high five. Yet we still need touch.

Touch also has a cultural component. As you travel around the world, you'll notice that other cultures don't value personal space as much as we do in the United States. (You might discover that when you're stuck in the middle of a teeming mob of people who don't mind pressing into you on all sides. Germophobes start to hyperventilate.) In the States, a common adult greeting is a hand-shake; in France, it's a kiss to both sides of the face; and in Japan, it's a simple bow. Different cultures, different customs, all normal.

IMPLICIT VS. EXPLICIT TOUCH

Loving touches may be implicit and subtle, requiring only a moment, like putting your hand on your mom's shoulder while you walk past her in the kitchen. Life is full of opportunities for implicit touches, like rubbing your little brother on the head as you walk through the room or sitting next to your family on the couch. These choices don't take much time, may require a little thought if they're not instinctive to you, and can go a long way in helping others feel connected to you. In contrast, explicit touches, such as a back rub, demand your full attention and obviously take more time and intentionality.

Everybody has different comfort levels when it comes to touch. Some people like to be touched; some don't. Some people only like certain people to touch them, and that's okay. That is their right. We need to be respectful of people's personal space, whether Touch is their love language or not.

So what feels comfortable and natural to you? Take the quiz below to identify your personal preferences. Write a ✓ or an X in the box for each touch that naturally fits that relationship.

RELATIONSHIP→ TOUCH ↓	PARENT	SIBLING	GRAND-PARENT	OTHER FAMILY MEMBER	FRIEND	GIRLFRIEND OR BOYFRIEND	STRANGER
HUG							
KISS ON THE CHEEK							
KISS ON THE LIPS							
BACK RUB							
FOOT MASSAGE							
PAT ON THE BACK							
WRESTLING							
HIGH FIVE							
SITTING CLOSE							
HOLDING HANDS							
HANDSHAKE							

Is Touch your love language? For those who answer yes, they like to be physically close to those they love. **Most of the people I know who feel loved through Touch have no doubt that this is their love language.** It's usually blindingly obvious to them.

SEX

Where does sex fit into this? We can't discuss physical touch as an emotional love language without addressing how this affects human sexuality.

Sex has the capacity to bond two people together closely. Sex also has the capacity to be empty, especially in our culture. We live in the aftermath of the sexual revolution, and it's left a trail of corpses (physical and emotional) in its wake.

The popular idea is that sex is a biological need on the same level as thirst. If you are thirsty, drink water. If you are hungry, eat food. If you have sexual desire, fulfill it. To many, sex has been reduced to mere copulation.

But deep down, none of us really believes that. We may drink water and eat food at any restaurant in the country, but having sex whenever, wherever, and with whomever does not meet the deep longing of the human soul for an exclusive sexual relationship.

Enter God's design: one man, one woman, for life. In other words, the establishment formerly known as "marriage." **Within the safety and security of the covenant of marriage, sex becomes an expression of love that is a dialect of the love language of Touch.** Because sex is so powerful, however, to treat it casually can leave lasting scars on the bodies and souls of people—especially people whose love language is Touch. It's like the difference between fireworks exploding in your hand versus in the sky. One's spectacular; the other can blow your fingers off.

How we express our human sexuality is no minor choice. It affects your physical and emotional health, as well as your sexual satisfaction, for years to come. As with any major choice in your life, this one is worth discussing with your parents. And if for some reason you cannot do this, look for another trusted adult, not just a buddy who will tell you what they think you want to hear. Different families have different faith backgrounds and values. (No, your parents may not be cool, but a tiny hint: they love you more than anyone else on this planet.)

// WARNING: ABUSE // No other love language has been more distorted than Touch. How sad.

As a little kid, you learned about appropriate/safe versus inappropriate/unsafe touch. Your parent hugging you: safe. Your doctor performing a routine check-up: uncomfortable but necessary. Physical or sexual abuse: inappropriate and unsafe. Abuse is typically done by a known, trusted adult who tries to convince you it's okay. It never is.

It's possible that you might have a friend struggling with wounds from past abuse. Maybe you are dealing with your own pain from something that happened to you. Sadly, children are often targets of abuse. The statistics are terrifying. Children are often silent about abuse for years. If they disclose as they get older, who will they usually tell? You, their friend.

How should you respond? For those teens who don't yet have a counseling degree or background in law enforcement, this is new territory to navigate—and the stakes are high. Here's my diehard, tried-and-true advice from decades of counseling: bring two trusted adults into the conversation—a parent and a school counselor, teacher, or pastor. Why? The abuser may be targeting other kids. The abused needs healing. And you as the friend will be a vital support, but you need support too.

CRISIS MODE

Almost instinctively, in a time of crisis we cling to one another. The more serious the situation, the more likely we are to hold on to or hug each other. Why? **Because physical touch is a powerful communicator of love, a tangible connection to another person.** When life hits code red (death of a family member, car crash, scary diagnosis, broken heart, emergency, or loss), we need to feel loved. We can't always change events, but with love, we can survive.

If your friend slips into crisis mode, especially if the person's love language is Touch, then you have to communicate your support with physical contact. If you've ever held a friend shaking or sobbing uncontrollably, then you already know what I mean. In moments of crisis, your words may mean little, but your touch will communicate your presence and care. Long after the crisis has passed, your friend will remember your physical embrace. In the same way, if you hold yourself stiffly away, that failure to touch will also never be forgotten.

ARE YOU LITERATE?

Can you read? (*Sigh,* you might be thinking. *What do you think I'm doing with this book?*) There's academic smart, which is book smart or reading smart—you can decode the words on the page. And then there's relational smart, which is emotional intelligence, a different brand of smart altogether. Someone might have a photographic memory for textbooks but might not be able to read people in relationships at all. In contrast, a savvy friend might struggle with academic work but be able to discern the relational, emotional climate between people. There are many ways to be smart.

When it comes to Touch, you need to be literate. You have to be able to . . .

• **Read people.** Some people crave physical touch. They light up when you hug them. Others stiffen up and withdraw if you slap them on the back. They want personal space, not contact. How well can you read the people close to you? You never want to project your own language onto someone else. Just because you enjoy being wrestled to the ground doesn't mean everyone else does. Respect people's preferences.

- **Read relationships.** Ask yourself, "What's appropriate in *this* relationship?" Touch varies from relationship to relationship: from your mom to your dad, from your older sister to your little brother, from a lifelong friend to a newer acquaintance, from the person you've been dating for two years to the person you started dating two days ago.
- **Read timing.** Do you want your mom to hug you at home? Do you want her to hug you in front of the entire school? Same touch, different context. If your friend has his arms crossed in anger, he doesn't want you to come within an inch. If he's hurting, your arm across his shoulder might communicate the solidarity he needs. Your girlfriend might want you to kiss her after your date (at least you hope). She might feel awkward if you kiss her at school. Read the climate.

GETTING PERSONAL

Can you think of someone you love whose primary language is Touch? Consider what your physical contact means to that person.

Those who are highly attuned to touch can sense love or affection in the slightest arm squeeze. Physical contact that wouldn't even register with most people has the potential to change their mood, brighten their day, and make them feel loved. A hug communicates love and affection to most people, but it *shouts* love to those who speak Touch.

Withholding physical touch from them has the potential to cause pain and anxiety that most nonnative speakers of their language cannot imagine. If someone avoids touching them, they take it personally. They may worry about the state of their relationships. They may feel lonely, even when surrounded by friends.

Here's the thought process: *Whatever there is of me resides in my body. To touch my body is to touch me. To withdraw from my body is to distance yourself from me emotionally.* Even if you can't relate to that, you can respect it, and you can find ways to deliver. So the next time your little brother wants to crawl all over you, let him. The next time your mom tries to put her arm across your shoulder, resist the urge to shrug her off. The next time your friend tries to give you a high five, don't leave him hanging. You don't have to change who you are, but you can be physically intentional.

PAUSE & PROCESS

1. Remember, of the five love languages, most people have one favorite. Is Touch your primary love language—does physical contact make you feel especially good or loved?
2. What types of physical touch do you consider affirming?
3. What kinds of touches make you feel uncomfortable?
4. To what degree did your parents speak the love language of Touch to you? To each other?
5. In your circle of friends, who are the "touchers"? Those who show their affection through touch often have the primary love language of Touch. In what ways might you reciprocate their love?
6. Looking back over the past day or two, what types of physical touches did you give to others? How did they seem to respond?
7. Whom have you encountered who seems to draw back from touching? Why do you think this is their natural response?

CHAPTER 6

AND YOU?

Michael split his childhood between Minnesota and Brazil, so he's an interesting mix of American and Brazilian. He can tolerate sub-zero temperatures and hold his own in lake sports, and he also has a sick touch on the soccer ball and loves strong coffee. He's fluent in English and Portuguese. In conversations with his brother, they slip seamlessly back and forth between the two languages. I'll be following along and then *bam!* off they go into Portuguese. And because of the similarities in languages, Michael can also comprehend a good amount of French and Spanish. He can't speak those perfectly, but he can follow a conversation.

But German? Or Russian? Or Japanese? Even Michael is lost in those languages. If you close your eyes and listen to someone speaking Swahili, for example, you realize that the sounds are totally different from English.

Whichever language you learned to speak first is your primary, native language. This is the language you understand best and can communicate most clearly in. **It's sometimes called your "heart" language—the language of your thoughts, feelings, and dreams.** Even those who learn to speak a second or third (or seventh) language will always be partial to their native tongue.

Same for the love languages. Of the five love languages, each of us has a primary love language. This is the one that speaks most deeply to us emotionally—our true heart language. Some of the others will sound and feel to our hearts as foreign as Arabic or Hungarian does to our ears.

So which one is your love language? Maybe you had an *aha!* moment the first time you glanced at a list of the five love languages. Maybe you read the chapters on Words or Service and realized, *Yes! That's exactly me.*

Then again, maybe it didn't happen that way.

For many people, discovering their primary love language is a challenge. The clues might not be that obvious. We shouldn't be surprised. After all, we're complex individuals. "Know thyself," the ancient aphorism says. "Just give me a minute!" we might reply.

There's a chance you might be bilingual, meaning two love languages speak equally to you. Now don't assume that's you just to be lazy. Do the work to figure out your love language. But if at the end of this chapter you still finish in a tie, that's okay. You're normal (well, kind of).

Two camps of people really struggle to discover their primary love language. In the first camp we meet the over-loved people. These lucky people have always felt loved, and their parents spoke all five love languages to them. As a result, they speak all five rather fluently, but they're not sure which speaks most deeply to them. They might say, "But I enjoy them all!" Yes—but which one can you not live without? Which is your true heart language?

In the second camp we meet the love-starved people. They grew up in dysfunctional homes and never felt secure in the love of their parents or the other significant adults in their lives. This whole love language business feels very new and uncertain to them. An act of service? They wouldn't know one if it smacked them in the face.

There's hope. Regardless of where you fall—in one extreme camp or the other, or somewhere in between—you have a primary love language. It may simply be lying dormant, waiting to be discovered or rediscovered.

Mission: to discover your primary love language. Here we go . . .

1. Observe your own behavior.

Start by asking yourself, "How do I typically express love and appreciation to other people?" What comes naturally to you? If you regularly hear yourself encouraging others verbally, then perhaps Words is your primary love language. You are doing for others what comes naturally to you and what you wish they would do for you. If your natural instinct is to throw your arms around someone, then maybe your go-to language is Touch. If you give thoughtful little gifts to others on birthdays or just because it's Tuesday, then maybe Gifts is your primary language. If you're the one who initiates getting all your friends together or inviting them over, then Time may be your love language. If you're observant, don't wait for someone else to ask, and just pitch in to help, then Service is likely your primary love language.

Note the qualifiers: *perhaps, maybe, likely.* Research indicates that about 25 percent of people speak one love language but wish to receive another. But for the majority of readers (75 percent), the language we speak most often is the one we also desire. We love others how we'd like to be loved.

2. Notice your own requests.

What do you ask others to do for you? If you regularly ask friends to help you with projects, then Service may be your love language. If your friend is going on a trip and you drop the hint for him to bring you something, then your love language is probably Gifts. If you tease, "Hey! Where's my hug?" then Touch is likely your primary language. If you regularly ask friends to go shopping with you, or on a road trip together, or over to your house for dinner, then you are asking for Time. If you fish for others' opinions and affirmation—"What do you think of my project? How does this look to you? What do you think about this?"—then you are asking for Words.

Our requests tend to indicate our emotional needs. Pay attention to what you request from others for clues about your primary love language.

3. Listen to your complaints.

What you complain about—out loud or in your head—can be very telling about your primary love language.

Justin and Kayla were assigned to do a group project together in American History. They sighed as soon as they saw their group— two workhorses (them) and three parasites (the others). They knew they'd do the majority of the work on the project, and they were right.

Justin said, "I can't believe no one else will put in the time on this. I even hosted a session at my house last Sunday evening, and only Kayla showed up." Can you tell from Justin's words what he most values? Time.

Our complaints reveal what matters most to us. If you complain that your friends don't have time for you during football season, then your love language is likely Time. If you grumble that all your friends forgot your birthday because only one gave you a gift, then your language is likely Gifts. If you complain that your dad's always trying to buy you off by bringing you gifts but he never even hugs you, then we can theorize that Gifts is his language and Touch is yours.

Our complaints reveal our deep emotional hurts. The opposite of what hurts you most is probably your love language. What do those closest to you do or say—or *fail* to do or say—that hurts you deeply? If, for example, the critical, judgmental words of your sister cause you the deepest pain, then your primary love language may be Words. Wounds in your native tongue really sting. If you received love in that language, then the hurt would lessen, and you would feel appreciated.

4. Ask the right questions.

Ask insightful questions—of yourself and others. Start by asking yourself the following questions:

- "What would the ideal boyfriend/girlfriend be like? If I could pick the ideal person, what would he/she be like?"
- "What do I want most in a friendship? What would an ideal friend be like?"
- "What do I like most about my friends? What do they say and do that makes them fun to be with?"

Your answers may be very enlightening and give you more clues about your primary love language.

5. Take the Love Languages Profile.

On page 121, you'll find the Love Languages Profile. You can also visit 5lovelanguages.com. This profile asks you to make choices between two options and to record your responses. The results will help you complete your mission: to discover your primary love language.

WHICH LOVE LANGUAGE IS THEIRS?

Discovering your own love language helps you understand why you feel more loved by and connected to certain people. Once you know your own language, you start to get your instincts—why you love others the way you do, why you're drawn to specific people, what you're looking for in a relationship. This self-knowledge can really help you in life. If you're a Touch person, then dating a person who avoids physical contact may leave you feeling emotionally starved. Or you'll have to learn how to really be assertive in asking for what you need: "Throw your arm around me so I don't feel like I'm floating away."

Once you know your own love language, your next mission, should you choose to accept it, is to learn other people's primary love languages. Don't picture an awkward guy consulting his clipboard so he can remember which of his friends needs to be verbally encouraged. After you do some intentional hunting and discover your friends' languages, this will become instinctive to you. You'll know who needs a surprise Starbucks delivery and who needs your open Saturday morning.

So how do you go about cracking the code? You can't simply text them and say, "What's your primary love language?" (Unless, of course, they also read the book and want to discuss it. Otherwise, you might get some weird emojis in their replies—maybe an eggplant, a shrimp, or one of those demonic-looking cats.) Here are a few techniques.

If you haven't yet, make a list of your primary relationships. This is your tribe—the five to ten people most connected to you.

Now start with the obvious. Just as you observed your own behavior to see how you naturally express love to others, watch them. If your dad loves your mom by serving her—building her a garden box, detailing her car, picking up her dry cleaning—then Service may be his preferred language. On the other hand, if your dad welcomes you home every day with a hug, then you might suspect his language is Touch. On the third hand (if you had one), if your dad publicly brags about you a lot, then Words might be his thing. For some people, this isn't a hard code to crack. For others who don't express love quite as freely or obviously, then they may have to watch more closely.

Just as you listened to your own complaints, listen to what your people say. Ask yourself, "What do they complain about most often?" If your sibling says, "I'm sick of picking up your towel. What do you ever do for me?" then his love language may be Service. If the person you're dating complains, "You never initiate a kiss. I feel like I'm chasing you," then you might wonder if Touch is his or her language. If you make your mom dinner for her birthday but she seems disappointed you didn't have a present for her to unwrap, then she's revealing the importance of gifts to her—a tangible little something to remind her of the day.

Just as you noticed your own request, now also listen closely to theirs.

- "Can we go for a walk around the lake?" Translation: Time.
- "Will you bring me something from your ski trip to Breckenridge?" Translation: Gifts.
- "Tell me how you like my new artwork." Translation: Words.

This isn't rocket science. It's not terribly difficult or painful. It just takes an observant mindset and a desire to learn more about the people you love.

Try asking questions too. For example, if your mom's birthday is coming up, instead of just mindlessly getting her another coffee mug, ask her what she wants. If she says . . .

- "I just want to spend the day with you." Translation: Time.
- "Surprise me with something little." Translation: Gifts.
- "The best gift would be if you help me with my garden." Translation: Service.

The final technique for learning someone's language is experimentation. This can be a fun secret mission. Pick one language and try it for a few days in a row, watching how the person responds. For example, for the first three days, focus on positive words. Say one really affirming statement to the person each day. Does that seem to fill the emotional tank? Then try one little gift per day—a $5 Starbucks card, then a funny bookmark, then self-sealing water balloons or a bag of gummy worms—and watch the response. Then spend some intentional, extended time with the person each day, and see how that fits. You'll be able to tell. If the person cringes at your hug, or doesn't jump at the chance to spend time together, or recycles your gift card, then you know that's not the answer, and you can try something else.

Experimentation requires some time, thought, and effort, but it's worth it. Rather than having five hundred lame, halfhearted, Facebook-only relationships, you can cultivate five or ten thriving relationships in which the others really know you and feel known by you.

PAUSE & PROCESS

1. If you already know your primary love language, how did you discover it? If you don't yet know your language, then take the Love Languages Profile on page 121 or at 5lovelanguages.com.
2. Review your list of primary relationships. Do you know each person's go-to love language? Fill in the chart on the next page to help you. In the left column, write the names of your closest people—your tribe. In each row, place a ✓ or an X in the box that matches their primary love language. Then write any brief notes that capture what you've learned about that person, evidence of their specific love language, or strategies you'd like to try.

RELATIONSHIP	#1: WORDS	#2: TIME	#3: GIFTS	#4: SERVICE	#5: TOUCH	NOTES EVIDENCE/STRATEGIES

CHAPTER 7

FAMILY

Family: You can't live with them; you can't live without them.

Honestly, who can annoy you better than your family? The way your dad eats corn on the cob—completely embarrassing, with corn and pepper and butter dripping down his chin. The way your little brother makes those obnoxious noises with his kneecaps—drives you insane. The way your mom yells at the ref who makes a call against you—you can hear it across the field. The way your sister is always making you late for school—come on. The way your parents hawk your grades, your phone, your driving, every little crevice of your life—seriously annoying.

No one can hurt you quite like your family. The closer someone is to you, the more access he or she has to your heart. Angry words can have enough truth in them to cut really deep. Within a family, we'll say hurtful words we'd never voice to or about a friend. We can be ruthless with those we love most. We know each other's weak spots, so we aim our verbal arrows precisely.

Yet no one can love you quite like your family. In healthy families, there's a sense of unconditional belonging. You might fail on stage, lose a girl/boyfriend, or get rejected by your friends, cut from the team, bullied, suspended, injured, or wrecked in any number of ways—but your family will still love you. No matter how big you mess up, they're still for you. When you fall, they're still there to pick you up.

Families were designed to be the basic caring unit of society. Family members are meant to love one another well. **Home should be that safe place where each individual is known, accepted, and loved unconditionally.** Families should give life a sense of stability. No matter what failure or rejection we experience outside the home, we should feel loved for who we are inside the home. In fact, "God sets the lonely in families."[7] Even if a family doesn't "look" perfect (dad, mom, 2.5 kids, the all-American dog, and a little white house with a red door), it can still be a healthy, vibrant, loving unit (even if it's single dad, or stepmom, or grandmother, or adopted parents, or half sibling, or blind cat, etc.). Even if it's not "perfect," it can still be really good.

But it's not always so. For many people, home is not a safe place, and some of the deepest wounds in life were inflicted by our families.

There's so much in life we can't control. If your family is dysfunctional or destructive, if you're a child of divorce, if you feel more wounded than loved at home, this is out of your control. You didn't cause it, and you can't fix it.

You can choose how you respond to it. In strained family relationships, applying the five love languages can help foster healing.

In healthy family relationships, applying the five love languages can enhance those bonds. You can respond to the most significant people in your life by speaking their primary love languages.

PARENTS

Breaking news: parents and teenagers don't have to clash on everything. It's not a moral or legal obligation. Some people expect that the parent–teen relationship will be strained, and it becomes a self-fulfilling prophecy. While that stretch of time before you leave home can have its share of explosions, as you're asserting your independence and your parents are weaning their control of your life and decisions, it doesn't have to be filled with tension, arguments, and disrespect. So if you're at peace with your parents, don't start a nuclear war on principle.

Instead, use peacetime for diplomacy. One of the best strategies for building your relationship with your parents is this sneaky little word: *honor*. One of God's original, top ten rules is "Honor your father and your mother, so that you may live long in the land the LORD your God is giving you."[8]

Ideally, love should flow from parent to child. When this consistently takes place and children genuinely feel loved, it is easy for them to honor their parents. However, kids who felt unloved, abandoned, or abused may struggle to honor their parents. Understandably.

Honoring your parents DOES NOT

1. mean painting over the past, pretending it didn't happen;
2. mean placing yourself in a position for more abuse (it's important to make and keep wise boundaries);
3. instantly heal a strained relationship;
4. suggest taking responsibility for your parents or even for the parent–child relationship.

But honor DOES enhance a good relationship and breathe some life back into a dying one. **When you choose to honor your parents, you pick out something specific and genuine that they did well for you, and you publicly thank and acknowledge them for that.**

We may feel deeply hurt by our parents. We may feel abandoned, disappointed, frustrated, and even depressed, but we can still express love to them. Love is an attitude that takes action.

FOR MISSING OR ABSENT PARENTS

It's a little trickier to honor a parent who's missing or dead. Okay, a lot trickier.

But it can still be done. If you have a parent who has died or who has been absent from your life, write a note—one to three sentences, or however much you can genuinely say—thanking your mom or dad for something specific. Even though your parent will never read your note, the process of writing it can serve as a helpful healing exercise for you.

"Dad, I remember the time when you ___. That meant so much to me."

"Mom, I wish I'd gotten more time with you. I miss you."

CASE STUDY: SAMUEL'S STORY

"My parents are workaholics. Both. I really don't spend that much time with them. Had a nanny when I was little. Spent my summers in camps. I guess the silver lining of that is I'm independent. Kind of forged my way on my own.

"Now I'm getting ready to leave for school. Carnegie Mellon in Pittsburgh. I know, it's *Pittsburgh*, but I like the computer science program. And I can't wait to be on my own.

"The funny thing is, now that I'm leaving for college, my parents suddenly want to spend time with me. It's like they realized there's a countdown, and our days are numbered. My mom's all about family dinners now, and my dad wants to watch football with me.

"What do I feel like saying? 'Where have you been the past eighteen years?' But I guess we're getting to that point now where I know they're not perfect. They tried, in their own messed-up way. I sure know what *not* do with my own family someday.

"So since they can't help but be the most awkward parents ever, I'm going to help them out. I'm trying to think of ways to reassure them that I really do love and appreciate them too.

"My mom's easy. The woman will not sit down. She's always serving, serving, serving us, like a Tasmanian devil on speed. So after dinner on Sunday evening, I got up and started the dishes, without being asked. By the time she got off the phone with my grandma, I was scrubbing the last pot. You should have seen her face when she walked into the kitchen.

"At first I was stumped with my dad, but then I realized he's a Time guy. He's always inviting me to watch a football game with him or go play nine holes of golf. So even though I don't particularly love golf, the other day I asked him, out of the blue, if he'd like to golf with me that weekend. You'd think I gave him a million dollars.

"And even though they're not Words people, I'm choosing to honor them verbally too. I picked out something specific to thank each of them for. I can't do one of those cheesy cards that says, 'You're the best dad in the whole world!' because that's just not true. So I wrote a simple card that thanked him for coming to my baseball play-offs. I told him that meant a lot to me. And I wrote my mom a note thanking her for packing me a healthy lunch every day. Not that I appreciated the kiwi and organic string cheese at the time, but I get it—that was her way of telling me she loved me. The least I can do is honor her for it."

SIBLINGS

There's so much potential in sibling relationships. After all, you share the same gene pool, and you grew up in the same home environment (in theory). No one else understands your parents' quirks quite like your siblings. No one else has as much shared history with you.

Listen to Jack's story: "From the time my brother, Aaron, and I were little, my mom drilled into us, 'Your brother is your best friend. He will always be your best friend. Ten years from now, will you still be friends with the kids from school, like Luke, Sawyer, and Connor? But for your whole life, your brother will be your best friend. Long after I'm dead, you'll still have your brother. This is a primary relationship in your life.'

"I mean, she brainwashed us. She was militant about this message, but I guess it worked. We're really different, but we've always been close.

"Once when I was five, these three older boys stole my Crocs at the playground. They were laughing and throwing my shoes to each other. By the time my mom got to the scene, little three-year-old Aaron had punched a seven-year-old kid and made him bleed. Why? He was defending me. He was only three, but he got it. He knew, 'You always fight for your brother. He's your best friend.'"

Not all siblings will be best friends, but they still have the potential to be tight or at least to look out for each other.

Listen to Annie's story: "Here's my history of best friends, from kindergarten through high school: Amy P., Amie W., Amy F., and then Aimee K. (Can you tell what girl's name was popular when I was growing up?) Today, they're all gone, scattered in different states, busy with their own lives. I read a Facebook update every now and then, but we're not close. The one constant? My brother, Nathan. He was there when I was born, when I was five, and when I was fifteen. Not like we always get along, but he's always there for me."

Though we're tempted to take our siblings for granted—after all, it's not like we chose each other—we should instead value them. How? By speaking each other's primary love languages.

SIBLING DISCLAIMERS

You always have to read the fine print, right? Like those commercials for new drugs that tell you 100 ways this drug can kill you and then encourage you to ask your doctor about the drug.

Not all siblings are close. In fact, some are distant or even estranged. If there's a legitimate reason for that–such as a history of abuse, or one sibling lives with a parent in Vermont and the other is with the other parent in Alaska–then you obviously need to adjust your expectations (and boundaries) for the relationship.

For some siblings, though, consider this your WAKE-UP CALL, an invitation to value the person you've often overlooked. It might take some time, thought, creativity, and effort, but enhancing that relationship with your sibling will be worth it. For life.

We've talked in depth about how to discover someone else's love language. (For a refresher course, see the "WHICH LOVE LANGUAGE IS THEIRS?" section in chapter 6, page 81.) Let's presume you applied that gray matter and figured out which love language your sibling speaks. Now it's time to brainstorm.

Let these ideas spark others for you. You'll find a mix of ideas here—some for little siblings, some for peer siblings, some for older siblings, some better suited to sisters or brothers, and so on.

HOW TO LOVE YOUR SIBLING

For the sibling who values Words

1. Send a text. In one sentence, tell what you really like about him, thank him for something he did for you, or say you're glad he's your brother.
2. Buy a card for a special occasion (birthday, graduation), and put some thought into the message.
3. Call your sister at college. Leave a message just telling her you were thinking of her.
4. Make a top ten list of your favorite things about your bro or sis.

For the sibling who values Time

1. Offer to babysit your brother's kid so he and his wife can go on a date.
2. Offer to help your sister with her science fair project.
3. Sit and play with your little brother. Follow his agenda. Let him pick what you play, and don't let anything distract you from it. (Don't look at your phone.)
4. Show up at your siblings' games, concerts, and meets. Be there in the crowd.

For the sibling who values Gifts

1. Surprise your brother with a Slurpee from 7-Eleven.

2. Frame a favorite picture for your sister, like the two of you hiking Mount Rainier in Washington last spring break.

3. Check your brother's Amazon Wish List, and buy him something from the list—for no reason, just because it's Friday.

4. Gift a song on iTunes—an easy click that clearly communicates, "I was thinking of you."

For the sibling who values Service

1. Offer to help your older brother with a house project, like painting, raking, or mulching.

2. Take your sister's car through the car wash. Then vacuum the interior.

3. Organize your little brother's playroom so he can find all his Legos and dinosaurs again.

4. Do your sister's chores during a week when she's feeling really busy.

For the sibling who values Touch

1. When you walk past your sister in the kitchen, pat her on the back.

2. When your little brother wants to sit hilariously close to you during a "scary" movie, let him in.

3. Take your sister for a pedicure.

4. Play tackle football with your brother in the backyard.

You'll notice that any one action has some crossover appeal. For example, if you take your sister to get a pedicure—if you wrap a gift certificate, it's a gift; if you watch her baby so she can go, that's an act of service; if you go together, that's the gift of your time; plus inherent in the pedicure is touch.

Think about your brother or sister, his or her love language, and his or her tastes, and use the ideas above to jump-start your own relationship-building campaign.

PAUSE & PROCESS

1. List the names of your immediate family members: mom, dad, siblings (and/or anyone else significant who lives with you). On a scale of 1 to 5, how loved do you feel by each of your family members?

    1 = barely loved, or not at all
    3 = somewhat loved
    5 = absolutely loved

2. Why did you rate each relationship as you did? Name some specific factors contributing to feeling loved/unloved.
3. What do you think is each family member's primary love language?
4. How effectively have you been speaking their primary love languages? Grade yourself using a similar scale. Cite specific examples.

    1 = I love the person but have no idea what language he/she likes.
    3 = I sometimes show love in his/her language.
    5 = I consistently speak his/her primary love language.

5. Brainstorm some strategies for expressing love to your immediate family members in the next week. Pick something simple and personal that you can realistically do for each person.

CHAPTER 8

ANGER AND APOLOGIES

What happened between Trey and Jasmine? They used to be inseparable buddies. If you asked either of them, they couldn't really say why they'd drifted apart. It just happened.

Something started in the fall. Trey was in a funk. Stuff at home was really stressful. His mom's hours at work got cut, his aunt and her baby were staying with them, some health junk with his grandma. Overload.

When Trey came to school, he just needed some space. He'd never needed space from Jas before. They'd always been best friends. When she walked in that morning, she was her usual, happy self, and he just didn't have the energy for a conversation. So he turned away.

Fine, she'd thought. *Must be a bad morning.* They had such a long history of friendship that his coldness rolled right off her.

The next morning, same thing. She was just so sincere, so attuned to him, and he didn't want anyone in his business, even her. So he put a little distance between them.

And she felt it.

Fine, she'd thought. *I'll give him space again.*

"Are you okay?" she asked him by the end of the week.

"Of course. Why? What's wrong with you?" His curt reply stung. *Fine*, she'd thought. *I'll keep my distance.*

And so the cycle began. He took his bad moods out on her

RANDOM FACT OF THE DAY

Did you know that anger is considered a secondary emotion?

Anger is triggered by something else—usually fear or sadness.

So when you feel angry, it's important to dig down to the true, primary emotion. Why do you feel angry? What are you really feeling?

For example, Bailey might lash out at her friend Libby in anger when she finds out Libby is moving. What's underneath the anger? Sadness. She'll miss her.

When Jose's frustration over his group project reaches an angry boiling point, he has to step back to see what's underneath that rage: fear that his group will get a bad grade and fear that he'll get stuck doing all the work.

When it comes to anger, there's often more to the story.

because she was his safe person. After a while, she couldn't *not* take it personally. She saw him acting normal around other people—everyone except her. What had she done? Or was it just her?

So she kept her distance. When she walked into a room, she didn't even make eye contact with him. She cheerfully greeted all their other friends and intentionally avoided him.

The frost grew to ice, and the ice hardened and thickened. No thaw came. If someone asked, neither knew why they'd grown apart. But now Jas felt only one thing toward Trey: anger. And Trey? He didn't know what he felt.

Sometimes our anger escalates out of control, creating distance in our relationships and eventually emotional dissonance with people we love. **Unresolved anger is like cancer in relationships.** Left unchecked, it kills.

Ever feel angry? That's normal. There's nothing wrong with experiencing anger. The issue is what you do with your anger.

- Do you deny it, stuffing it down inside you, until you'll someday erupt like a volcano, spilling hate-lava on the people around you?
- Do you suffer in silence and withdraw from others, meanwhile simmering inside?
- Do you let your anger control you?
- Do you explode on people?
- Do others tiptoe gingerly around you so as not to ignite your short fuse?
- Do you grow irrational, raging and verbally lashing out at others?
- Or do you process your anger productively, communicating how you feel and working through your anger toward resolution?

Sadly, many people never learn how to process anger properly. As a result, relationships become a battlefield. "You fired the first shot!" "No, you did!" Yet love and uncontrolled anger can't coexist. Love seeks the well-being of the other, while uncontrolled anger burns relationships and the people in them.

Many of us can remember family outings that were spoiled not by bad weather but by our parents' petty little fights. How many birthdays and holidays felt miserable because of anger run rampant?

SCHOOL OF ANGER MANAGEMENT

To feel anger is to be human. So what's a human to do with these intense feelings of anger? Enroll in the School of Anger Management, and follow these five tips.

1. Admit it—anger's real.

Whenever you're in a close relationship with someone, anger is inevitable. Whether the person said or did something wrong to you or there's a misunderstanding brewing between you, you'll get angry. There's nothing inherently, morally wrong about anger. It's a clue that something feels unfair or unjust to you.

We need to give ourselves permission to be angry. Don't deny it or pretend that you're fine when you're not.

And we need to give those closest to us permission to be angry too. In some relationships, there's a power differential. One person is dominant and feels the freedom to rage. The other person feels weaker and pressured to hide anger. That's not fair or healthy, and it's not a recipe for a successful relationship.

Ask yourself, "Do others feel comfortable telling me how they really feel?" If your mom or your little brother or your friend feels intimidated by you, too scared to speak up if something's wrong, then something's wrong.

If we want authentic relationships, then we need to be open to hearing what those we love really think and feel. We need to give them freedom to be themselves.

2. Say it—express your anger.

Don't play "Guess My Mood." When you're angry, don't act all passive-aggressive about it, throwing off icy-cold vibes and expecting others to read your thoughts. **If someone has done or said something to upset you, express that you're angry and why.** The other person deserves to know why there's distance between you. That's the only way you two can remedy the problem and repair the relationship. And if this person is in your tribe—those five to ten people closest to you—then that relationship is worth repairing.

3. Guard it—follow ground rules.

Whether it's ultimate fighting or a military battle, every conflict has ground rules. Same for interpersonal conflicts. The unhealthy, out-of-control venting of anger is always destructive, unacceptable, and inappropriate. An emotional explosion makes things worse, and then you have to deal with the debris from that tirade before you can even begin to constructively address the incident that triggered the anger.

So let's say that your friend insulted you. How should you respond?

Option 1: "When you said _____, that hurt. That wasn't cool."

Option 2: "You are the most selfish, cruel, narcissistic human being in the history of the world." Then cross/jab/uppercut to the face.

All in favor of option 1? Option 2 violates several ground rules. First, it's hyperbole (gross exaggeration for dramatic effect—remember that literary term?). Really, is the person worse than Hitler? Why do we resort to such extremes? Second, you attacked the *person* rather than focusing on the *behavior*. Third, well, that wasn't self-defense; it was physical abuse.

When you verbalize your anger, pinpoint the specific action or words that upset you, and tell the person how it made you feel.

4. Ask—don't attack.

There are two (or more) sides to every story. You see things from one perspective: yours. But there may be more to the story than what you see and know. Don't fly off the handle and attack the other person. Ask questions, and give the other person a chance to explain her perspective.

Sydney overheard her little brother talking to his friend. She wasn't exactly eavesdropping, but his words caught her attention—and made her blood boil. "She is *always* late. . . . I know, we rush and then just sit and wait for her." Sydney immediately assumed Austin was talking about her. Her parents made her drive Austin to school and sometimes even to his practices, and here he was complaining about her? She felt like telling him off. He could find his own rides!

While she waited for Austin to get off the phone, she rehearsed her nasty response to him. Fortunately, she simmered down from furious to red-hot-mad and asked him, "Who's always late, Austin?"

Austin looked up at her in surprise. "Mrs. Ellis, my chemistry teacher. She gives us this ridiculous amount of homework and then never bothers to grade it. Takes her like a month to get anything back to us. Why, Syd?"

"Oh." Sydney's anger dissipated. *Note to self: don't assume*, she thought.

You can't assume you know someone's thoughts and motives, and it's easy to misinterpret actions. Ask.

5. Don't discard the relationship—repair it.

Some relationships in life are disposable. It's okay if you don't keep in touch with that kid who sat beside you in kindergarten and picked his nose constantly. It's okay if you say goodbye to that person you were dating who was clearly so wrong for you. But for those people closest to you, it's worth fighting for and repairing your relationships.

Nobody's perfect. Not even you (*especially* you). Because relationships are made up of imperfect people, they're messy. People make mistakes and hurt each other. People do and say awful things. **No relationship survives long-term without forgiveness.**

Anger serves an important purpose in relationships. It flags something wrong, like a flashing warning light. When someone hurts you, call it like it is. Don't pretend it didn't hurt. It did! Direct, loving confrontation opens the door to constructive conversation and problem solving. Hear each other out, resolve the issue, learn from the experience, and move on together. Healthy relationships need lots of apologies and forgiveness (more on that to come).

THE SCHOOL OF APOLOGIES

The art of apologizing is not easy. It doesn't come naturally to most of us, but we can learn it. And it's worth the effort. We all make mistakes. The question is, what do we do after we've made a mistake?

A true apology can bring closure to tensions, conflicts, and hurt feelings that have been sore spots for months, even years. It can break down barriers faster than any other words or actions can.

Apologies must be sincere. Anyone can tell when an apology is obligatory, forced, or fake. Let's practice the language of genuine apologies.

1. "I'm sorry."

Lead off with these two words.

Then be specific. "I'm sorry for _____." The more details you give, the better you communicate to the other person that you understand exactly what hurt him. By being specific, you also give the other person a chance to clarify. If you say, "I'm sorry for not spending time with you at the party," your friend might surprise you and say, "Actually, that's not why I'm mad. You had told me you wanted to ride together and introduce me to someone, and then you acted like I wasn't even there."

No "buts." Words of sincere regret need to stand alone. Never add the word *but*. ("I'm sorry I said all those mean things to you, but you were irritating me.") That shifts the blame to the other person. That's not an apology; it's an attack.

No excuses. When you follow an apology with an excuse, you cancel out the apology. ("I'm sorry you got stranded at school, but Will said we should just go.")

"I'm sorry" focuses on how your behavior caused the other person pain. Start with those two, simple, powerful words: "I'm sorry."

2. "I was wrong."

Why is it so hard for some of us to admit, "I was wrong"? As if being wrong means we're weak? Too often we rationalize. Justify. Gloss over *what* we did and focus on *why*. Blame others.

That totally undermines an apology. For many people, those three words, "I was wrong," really communicate that an apology is sincere.

> "MY DAD NEVER ADMITS HE WAS WRONG. HE'S SUCH A HYPOCRITE. HE'LL BLAME MY MOM, MY BROTHER, ME, THE WEATHER, TRAFFIC. IT'S ALWAYS SOMEONE ELSE'S FAULT. SO I KNOW EVEN WHEN HE SAYS 'I'M SORRY,' WHAT HE REALLY MEANS IS 'I'M SORRY YOU MADE ME DO THAT.' JUST FOR ONCE IN MY LIFE, I'D LOVE TO HEAR HIM ADMIT HE WAS WRONG."
>
> —JONATHAN

If you're choking over these words, then practice. You can do it! "I was wrong."

3. "How can I make this right?"

If you lost your sister's iPhone—buy her a new one.

If you ditched your friend on Friday night—hang out on Saturday.

If you lied to your coach—go tell him the truth.

For some wrong actions, there's an obvious remedy. The idea of restitution, or making things right, is deeply embedded in our human psyche. We all have an internal scale of fairness, and when things have been off-balance, we want to make them even again. Knowing the love languages of your tribe can help you restore justice and love in a relationship. You can express restitution in the other person's primary love language.

For Words people, tell them how incredible they are and how much they mean to you, in conjunction with your apology.

For Service people, prove you're sincere by doing something for them, such as cleaning out their car, doing their laundry, or mowing the lawn.

For Gifts people, give something that shows you were thinking of them and that communicates "I'm sorry" deeply.

For Time people, give your undivided attention while you apologize.

For Touch people, an apology without physical contact feels insincere, so bridge the physical distance between you and give them a hug.

Speaking an apology in someone's love language communicates that you genuinely care about the person.

Now there are some hurts you just can't make right. Restitution is impossible. That changes the question from "How can I make this right?" to "How can I show you I still love you?" If you betray your best friend, or publicly humiliate your dad, or cheat on your girlfriend, you can't exactly make that right. But in the context of your apology, you can communicate that you love the person.

4. "I won't do that again."

The technical term for this is "repentance." *Repent* means to turn around or change one's mind. It's choosing to make a change.

> "MY BOYFRIEND FLIRTS WITH OTHER GIRLS. LIKE OPENLY FLIRTS. HE CLAIMS HE'S JUST BEING FRIENDLY, BUT I DON'T READ IT THAT WAY. WHAT UPSETS ME MOST IS THAT HE DOES IT OVER AND OVER AGAIN. MY FEELINGS ARE HURT, WE TALK IT THROUGH, HE APOLOGIZES, HE PROMISES NEVER TO DO IT AGAIN, AND THEN HE DOES IT AGAIN."
>
> —ABBY

What Abby is looking for (besides a new boyfriend) is repentance, not a 5,000th apology.

True repentance begins in the heart. We realize that we've hurt someone we love. We don't want to continue hurting the person and decide to change. We verbalize that decision to the person offended. We don't minimize our behavior but accept full responsibility for our actions.

What people who have been hurt want to know is, "Do you intend to change, or will this happen again next week?" The answer to that question depends on repentance.

5. "Will you forgive me?"

Requesting forgiveness does three vital things:

- It indicates that you want to see the relationship restored.
- It shows that you realize you did something wrong.
- It gives the offended person a measure of control.

You can't force other people to forgive; they have to choose. The future of your relationship depends on the other person's decision.

That helps restore the balance of power in the relationship.

To some people, without that request for forgiveness, the apology falls flat—no matter how many times you say "I'm sorry" or "I was wrong" or "I'll make it up to you" or "I'll never do it again."

If you want healthy relationships, then you need to learn the art of apologies. You'll need to become fluent in those five key phrases and add a big dollop of sincerity.

PAUSE & PROCESS

1. Recall a time when you felt really angry at someone close to you. What happened? How did you process your anger? What can you learn from that experience?
2. Recall a time when someone else was really angry with you. What happened? What can you learn from that experience?
3. In what ways can anger help in a relationship?
4. When is anger harmful?
5. Review the five tips from the School of Anger Management. Which do you struggle with most? How can you work on this?
6. Review the School of Apologies section. When you've been hurt, which of those five phrases means the most to you? Why?
7. Which phrase do you most need to practice?
8. Why are apologies and forgiveness vital to any healthy, lasting relationship?

CHAPTER 9

LOVE IS A CHOICE

'm going to let you in on a secret.

This is like having the answer key to the final exam the day before the big test. This is a hard lesson that takes some people decades to figure out—and some never do. They just stumble from relationship to relationship, brokenhearted, dazed, and disappointed. If you learn this now, you'll save yourself pain and build stronger relationships. Enough of the sales pitch? Okay, here's the secret:

The feeling of being in love doesn't last.

Well, you might argue, *that might be true for other people, but not for me. You don't know what my relationship is like.* False. No exceptions. This is an ironclad, biological/emotional/psychological fact: *the high of being in love does not last.* For most people, that feeling you get (like a high) from being newly in love lasts up to two years. Maybe less. After that, the emotions calibrate toward normal, and you have to make a decision: do you scrap the relationship and move on to the next emotional high, or do you figure out what real love looks like?

Now I'm not saying you should date the same person for ten years just to prove you're not a quitter. There's no prize for gutting it out in the wrong dating relationship. Depending on your dating philosophy (likely colored by your parents' advice), you may find that dating different people helps you learn a lot about yourself and how to navigate relationships. I'm not arguing for being betrothed (old-school engagement) at age fourteen. What I *am* saying is that once you land in a long-term relationship, whether that's at age 18 or 28 or 58, if you want it to last, then you must have realistic expectations.

Those expectations are rooted in a true definition of love. Love isn't two starry-eyed lovers being drawn together by a magical, gravitational force, while a romantic soundtrack plays in the background. **Love is not a feeling; it's a choice.** Love isn't about getting everything you want and need and making sure you always feel happy. Love is a choice to meet someone else's needs, to sacrifice for another, to want what's best for the other—even when it's hard.

CASE STUDY: ELLA AND RYAN

"You two are perfect together," all their friends said. Ella and Ryan agreed. From the moment they'd met in college, they were magnetically drawn to each other. Ryan has a huge personality, massive heart, and genuine smile; he is extroverted and naturally draws people to him. Ella is a quiet beauty, a fantastic listener, always up for whatever adventure Ryan dreams up. They fell in love.

Two years later, they got married.

Two years after that, they were contemplating a divorce.

Why? What happened during those two years of marriage? Nothing earth-shattering—no collapse of the world economy or septic fumes underneath their first apartment. What happened? Life happened. They both had demanding jobs. They spent less and less time together. They bought a too-expensive car and a too-pricey vacation, then had to work overtime to pay them off. They got distracted by grad school, work, family, bills, the daily grind. Meanwhile the emotional high of being in love wore off, and when their feelings faded, they concluded they weren't meant to be together.

Ella and Ryan faced a decision: should they cut their losses, or fight for their marriage? If they dissolved their marriage, they'd likely fall into the same pattern again with someone else: fall in love and then find that staying in love takes a lot more work. Different partner, same pattern.

They decided to try to salvage their marriage. Ryan wasn't so sure at first. Ella's quiet resolve willed them to try again. The first step for them was to recognize that they weren't meeting each other's emotional needs. Their love tanks were empty. The second step was to discover each other's love languages and then work to speak love to each other in those languages.

Once Ryan learned that Ella needed Words, he directed more of his verbal energy toward her. He'd been talking to and about everyone except Ella. From the moment she'd met him, his words had drawn her to him. Once she started receiving loving words again, she transformed. The bitter, exhausted version of her faded, and an energized, loving Ella returned.

Once Ella knew that Ryan needed Time, she stopped volunteering her time out to others so freely. Sure, her friend might like her company while she painted her house, but her husband needed her company. Sure, she could take on one more photography shoot, but more than the extra paycheck, her marriage needed her presence. That time together made Ryan feel loved again.

Ella and Ryan are the lucky ones. By learning at age twenty-four what real love looks like, they saved their marriage. The emotional high of falling in love doesn't last. **Falling in love and staying in love are two different things.** And real, lasting love takes work. Someday you may fall in love and get married. You'll learn that "in love" feelings don't last but real love can.

CASE STUDY: THE WOODS FAMILY

Alexis was so scarred by her parents' marriage that she wasn't sure she'd ever want to get married. Her parents detested each other. They stayed together for one reason: the kids. And everyone knew it. Mr. Woods lived upstairs; Mrs. Woods lived on the first floor. They exchanged checks to pay the bills and spoke very rarely and only about business matters: "Did you pay the utility bill? Alexis has a swim meet on Saturday; can you drive her? Stop parking on my half of the garage." They loved their kids but clearly did not enjoy each other. In public, they kept their distance. At Alexis's meets, they sat apart.

They seemed to get the concept of sticking together but missed the memo about love. Many relationships, left untended, die a slow, hard death. But simply gutting it out doesn't save love.

Once Alexis left for college, she had a more objective perspective on her parents' marriage. She could see them as hurting individuals, too stubborn to learn each other's love languages. She could see they wanted to do what's right, but they got stuck on the how. After some counseling work of her own, Alexis learned that real love takes commitment but is about more than commitment. She started spending more time with her aunt and uncle, who have a healthy marriage, and that helped redefine love in Alexis's mind. By learning what love is not—boring, suffocating, duty-only, lifeless, monotonous—Alexis began to learn what love is. And she began to learn what love requires—communicating in another's language.

LOVE IS AN ACT OF THE WILL

Love is a function of the mind/will/heart—not the emotions/hormones/feelings. In fact, feelings can be very misleading. "The heart is deceitful above all things and beyond cure. Who can understand it?"[9]

"Do what feels right" and "just follow your heart" are two

common pieces of advice you'll hear in life, but they won't serve you well. No, your feelings can lead you straight off a cliff. Do you think your mom *feels* like cooking dinner for your family yet again? Will you always *feel* like loving your family? If your heart gives you bad advice ("Shoplift those jeans. Make fun of your friend behind her back. Cheat on your boyfriend."), then sometimes you have to politely tell your heart, "Shut up! I'll check back with you later."

Actions precede feelings. Your heart is a shameless follower. If you choose to do what you know is best, then your heart will eventually follow. Let's say your relationship with your sister is strained. Maybe you know she's a Words person. You can follow your heart and say something cruel and cutting, which feels good for about three seconds, or you can choose to love her with Words and say something affirming to her. She might look at you in shock, and your heart may resist, but you just started filling her emotional tank. If you keep choosing to love, then your heart will eventually follow. Eventually you'll feel like loving her—and you'll be glad you chose to.

Our emotions are often at war with each other, competing for dominance. It's an epic, internal clash. When it comes to loving those closest to you, choose love—don't follow your fickle feelings.

WHAT IF IT'S HARD?

Here's a common objection I hear: "But Dr. Chapman, what if the other person's love language doesn't come naturally for me?"

My standard reply: "So?"

My wife's love language is Service. You know what makes her really happy? When I vacuum the carpet.

Vacuuming does not come naturally to me. More accurately, *I hate it*. My mom used to make me vacuum. When I was in middle school and high school, she never let me go out on Saturdays until I'd vacuumed the entire house. Back in the day, I vowed, "When I get

out of here, there's one thing I'm never going to do again: vacuum."
But I still vacuum. Regularly. For one reason only: because I love
my wife. You couldn't pay me to vacuum a house, but I do it for love.
And my wife knows that when I vacuum, it doesn't come naturally to
me, so it's an even greater expression of love.

Ultimately, your personal comfort isn't the issue. Love is something you do for someone else. Once you discover the primary love
language of someone close to you, you choose to speak it—whether
or not it feels natural or comfortable for you. Even when it's not 100
percent convenient. You may not get warm, fuzzy feelings while
you're doing it, but that's fine. It's not about you. Love is a choice.

PAUSE & PROCESS

1. The high of falling in love doesn't last. How does knowing that
   help you set realistic expectations for your current and future dating relationships?
2. Love is an act of the will. Describe a time you chose to love—even
   though you didn't feel like it.
3. The heart has been described as deceptive. How have you experienced this to be true?
4. Which should you follow—what you *feel* is right or what you *know*
   is right? Why?

CHAPTER 10

Q&A: A CANDID CHAT WITH DR. CHAPMAN

Q. *What if I can't figure out my primary love language?*
A. Don't give up. You've got one.

If you haven't yet, take the Love Languages Profile on p. 121 or at 5lovelanguages.com. It's a quiz that should give you insight into your wiring.

You can also use the process of elimination. Maybe when you read the description of a certain language, you thought, *That is so not me.* Cross that one off, and you're down to four. You should be able to narrow it to two or three options simply by the process of elimination.

Also, in chapter 6, I described some strategies for deducing your love language:

1. Observe your own behavior. How do you most naturally express love to others?
2. Notice your own requests. What do you ask others to do for you?
3. Listen to your complaints. What bugs you in relationships?
4. Ask yourself questions: What would an ideal dating relationship be like? What do I value most about my friends?

These strategies give you clues to help you discover your primary language.

Q. *Will my primary language change over time?*

A. No. It's embedded in you, like eye color. Your primary love language will most likely stay with you for life. It's like many other personality traits that develop early and stay consistent. For example, the little kid who neatly organizes his Legos in colored bins will likely keep his homework organized in high school. That's a fixed personality trait.

However, sometimes life skews the love languages temporarily. Let's say you're going through a really stressful semester academically. You can hardly keep up with your homework, let alone sleep. Your primary love language might be Words, but during this busy season, Service might become extremely attractive to you. While you still appreciate hearing "I love you," when your family does things to help you, you feel super grateful. During that semester, it might seem like Service is eclipsing Words for you, but that's not true. If your family stopped loving you with Words, then your love tank would drain to empty fast.

A crisis can also skew your language. For example, if a parent or close friend dies, you may receive (and appreciate) more hugs than ever, even though Touch isn't your primary language. During times of grief, Touch communicates love silently and powerfully. So while Touch isn't normally your thing, for that intense season of grief, it might mean a lot to you.

While your love language will be constant throughout life, it may look a little different at different stages. Ten years ago you might have loved finding a little note with a joke in your lunch bag, getting a lollipop as a surprise treat, or snuggling with your parents. Today, your tastes are different, though your love language is the same.

Q. *Does this concept work on everyone?*

A. Yes. *Everyone.* From your three-year-old cousin Charlie to your great-grandma Betty and everyone in between. Every person has a love tank and feels especially loved through one primary language.

Daniel grew up with a lot of love. No, his family wasn't perfect, but even though his parents divorced when he was only four, they were intentional about loving him. His parents gave him huge doses of his primary language (Touch) and also sprinkled in the other four, determined to communicate to their son that he was unconditionally loved. The result? Daniel is a well-adjusted seventeen-year-old with healthy relationships of his own.

In contrast, Mia's parents loved her, but they were terrible about expressing it. They're what we might call "emotionally constipated." Maybe Mia knew in her mind she was loved, but she sure didn't feel it. In fact, she felt like her parents' favor totally depended on her performance. If she excelled at something, they were happy with her, and if she failed or struggled, they were cold to her. By the time Mia was a sophomore, she was looking for love in all the wrong places. And her empty love tank translated into other problems too: anger, discipline issues, even slipping grades.

So yes, this concept applies to *everyone,* and it affects almost *everything*. Empty love tank? Problems galore. Full love tank? Those healthy relationships, in which you give and receive love, affect your self-image, self-worth, and satisfaction and success in life.

Q. *What if some languages just feel really awkward to me?*
A. Fear not, every love language can be *learned.* You may just have to work at it.

Think of how you're wired academically. To some people, reading is fun and easy. To others, it's torture. Yet in school, even if reading is unnatural for you, you're expected to read. Same with algebra. Some minds are wired that way, and some students have to work really hard just to pass their core math classes. Now that doesn't mean those math-challenged students should aim to be MIT math professors, but they do have to work hard enough to get through the requirements.

We can apply that same logic to the love languages, with a twist. Just because something doesn't feel natural doesn't mean you can't—or shouldn't—learn it. In fact, you have a real motivation for learning it. By learning to speak the love language of someone close to you, like your big brother, you are investing in a lifelong relationship with him. Ten years from now, when you have to schlep your stuff to a new apartment, guess who's going to show up to help you move? Your brother. Twenty years from now, when your car breaks down and your kid has a broken leg and your pipes just burst, guess who's still a part of your life? Your bro.

So even if it feels a little awkward to you, it's totally worth it. Anytime you invest in people, you reap lasting rewards.

Start small. If your brother's primary language is Words, don't start by delivering a thirty-minute speech about him. Begin with a text or a single comment, short and sweet:

- "I'm glad we spent time together today."
- "You are rock solid at penalty kicks."
- "Cool shirt. It looks good on you."

Each of those was seven words. I know you can manage seven words, and with a little willpower and practice, you can intentionally launch sincere words his way on a regular basis. The result? A close bond with the guy who's going to jump-start your car in two decades.

Q. *Where did the 5LL concept come from?*
A. Years of counseling experience. Over time, I started to notice a pattern. What makes one person feel loved doesn't necessarily make another person feel loved. I read over my notes and tried to answer this question: "When someone wants to feel loved, what does that person really want?" The answers fell into five categories, which I called the five love languages.

Once I started teaching this 5LL concept in workshops, I saw the lights go on for people. They realized why they'd been missing each other emotionally. Once they started applying the 5LL concept, they radically changed the emotional climate of their relationships.

I wrote the 5LL in a book form, hoping to help people whom I'd never have a chance to meet. The book has now sold more than ten million copies in English and has been translated into around forty languages around the world, so I feel like it struck a chord with people, which is very satisfying to me as a counselor.

Q. Why is the 5LL concept so important to relationships?
A. Our deepest emotional need is to feel loved. It's hardwired into us as humans. We don't need to feel loved by the strangers and casual acquaintances in our lives, like the mail carrier and local Starbucks barista, but we do need to feel loved by those closest to us. Our tribe. Our family. Our tight friends. When we feel loved, we can weather a lot of storms in life, and the future still looks sunny. When we don't feel loved, we feel alone and rejected, and the future looks dark.

Here's the disconnect: even if we are loved by people, we may not *feel* loved. Someone could be shouting love to you in Gifts or Time, but you may be deaf to those. And you may be shouting Service to others who are deaf to that language.

The secret is communicating in others' languages. Once families and friends begin speaking each other's primary love languages, they are surprised by how quickly their emotions turn positive. With full love tanks, they can process conflicts; create a positive, emotional climate; and work together, support, and encourage each other.

And when you *feel* loved, you can take on the world.

Q. What if I speak other people's love languages, but they don't reciprocate?

A. Love is a choice. We can request love but can't demand it. There may be reasons why someone can't or won't speak your love language. If your boyfriend's family uses words only to fillet each other, then he may be reluctant to use words toward you. What's the root of the problem?

Ultimately, you may drift apart from someone who refuses to speak your language. Even if you feel really close to a certain friend, if there's a basic disconnect between you, then that may be a friend for that season, not your best friend for life. You wouldn't want to marry and spend the rest of your life with someone who refuses to try to learn your language. And vice versa.

For those people who are fixtures in your life, though (your family), you may need to just keep loving them, even if it's not reciprocated. Let's say your sister is widowed at age 29, leaving her a single mom with two little girls. She's not going to have much left to give you, and that's okay. You can keep loving her, knowing that your emotional needs will be met elsewhere.

Love is a choice. Love is a verb.

THE 5 LOVE LANGUAGES PROFILE

W hat's your love language? Do you already have a hunch? Or no clue at all? Either way, the following quiz will help you determine your primary love language.

The profile includes thirty pairs of statements. Read each pair, and choose the one that better reflects your preferences. In some pairs, both might be true, so choose which is even more *you*. For accurate results, you can only pick one. In the right column, circle the letter that corresponds with the statement you choose.

The profile statements describe the people you love. When we think of the five love languages, we might immediately think of romantic relationships. However, as we've discussed throughout the book, this applies to all your close relationships: siblings, parents, boyfriend/girlfriend, close friends, mentors, and so on.

Take the profile when you're relaxed. Don't rush. After you've made your thirty selections, go back and count the number of times you chose each letter. List the results in the matching spaces at the end of the profile, and then read how to interpret your score.

Good luck, and have fun!

1
I like to spend one-on-one time with people.   B

I feel loved when someone gives practical help to me.   D

2
I like it when people give me gifts.   C

I really enjoy hanging out with people close to me.   B

3
I feel loved when someone I'm close to puts an arm around me.   E

I feel loved when I receive a gift from someone I'm close to.   C

4
Gifts are symbols of love that are important to me.   C

I feel loved when people affirm me.   A

5
I like to spend time with friends and family.   B

I like to receive little gifts from friends and family.   C

6
Words of acceptance mean a lot to me.   A

I know someone loves me when he or she helps me.   D

7
I like to receive affirming notes and texts.   A

I like to be hugged.   E

8
I like being with and doing activities with friends and family.   B

I like it when kind words are spoken to me.   A

9
What someone does affects me more than what he or she says.   D

Hugs make me feel connected and valued.   E

10 I value praise and avoid criticism.   A

Several small gifts mean more to me than one large gift.   C

11 I feel close to someone when we are talking or doing something together.   B

I feel closer to friends or family when they touch me often.   E

12 I appreciate when people compliment my achievements.   A

I know people love me when they do things for me that they don't enjoy doing.   D

13 I like when my friends and family greet me with a hug.   E

I like it when people listen to me and show genuine interest in what I'm saying.   B

14 I feel loved when friends and family help me with jobs or projects.   D

I really enjoy receiving gifts from friends and family.   C

15 I enjoy when people compliment my appearance.   A

I feel loved when people take time to understand my feelings.   B

16 I feel secure when someone close to me is touching me.   E

Acts of service make me feel loved.   D

17 I appreciate the many little things that people do for me.   D

I value gifts that people make for me.   C

18 I really enjoy the experience of one-on-one, undivided attention.   B

I really enjoy it when someone does some act of service for me.   D

19

I feel loved when people do things to help me.   D

I feel loved when people touch me.   E

20

For my birthday, I feel loved when I receive a gift.   C

For my birthday, I feel loved when someone speaks meaningful words   A
to me.

21

I know someone is thinking of me when he or she gives me a gift.   C

I feel loved when someone helps me with my chores.   D

22

I like to go places with people I'm close to.   B

When I like someone, I make contact with the person (hug, shove, high   E
five, etc.).

23

I appreciate it when someone listens patiently and doesn't interrupt me.   B

I appreciate it when someone remembers special days with a gift.   C

24

I like knowing that people are concerned enough to help with my   D
daily tasks.

I enjoy full-day adventures or trips with someone close to me.   B

25

Getting a kiss from a parent or older relative makes me feel loved.   E

Receiving a gift for no special reason from a parent or older relative   C
makes me feel loved.

26

I like to be told that I'm appreciated.   A

I like for people to look at me when we're talking.   B

27

I like to sit close to people I enjoy being with.   E

I appreciate when someone tells me how attractive I am.   A

28
| Gifts from people I'm close to are always special to me. | C |
| I feel good when someone I'm close to touches me. | E |

29
| I feel loved when someone enthusiastically does some task I've requested. | D |
| I feel loved when I'm told how much I'm appreciated. | A |

30
| I need to be touched every day. | E |
| I need words of affirmation every day. | A |

TOTALS

A _____

B _____

C _____

D _____

E _____

CODE

A. Words

B. Time

C. Gifts

D. Service

E. Touch

WANT MORE?

- To learn more about the love language of **Words,** go to ch. 1, p. 21.
- To learn more about the love language of **Time,** go to ch. 2, p. 35.
- To learn more about the love language of **Gifts,** go to ch. 3, p. 47.
- To learn more about the love language of **Service,** go to ch. 4, p. 57.
- To learn more about the love language of **Touch,** go to ch. 5, p. 67.

INTERPRETING YOUR QUIZ SCORES

Which language received the highest score for you? This is your *primary* love language. If two tied, then you are *bilingual* and have two primary languages. If a second language scored almost as high as your primary language, then that means you have a *secondary* language, and both are important to you. The highest possible score for any single love language is 12, and the total is 30. Your mix might look like this: 11 for your primary, 9 for your secondary, and then 5, 3, and 2 for the others. Or you could have a 12, followed by a distant 6, 5, 4, and 3. What you won't have is an even split (all scores of 6)—that would be highly rare.

Whatever your primary language is, don't write off the others. Your friends and family may express (and need) love in these languages, and you should know this about them. As we speak each other's love languages, we feel known and connected.

ACKNOWLEDGMENTS

GARY

I am indebted to Paige Haley Drygas and the research and writing she invested in this book. In addition, I want to thank my editor, Pam Pugh, for making it communicate even more effectively to a teenage audience. Finally, I am grateful for the many teens who through the years have shared their joys and struggles with me.

PAIGE

Thank you

To Gary Chapman, who let me have fun with his profound 5LL concept.

To CH, who keeps hiring me for some reason.

To my WA soccer girls, who made me fall in love with working with teens.

To my church family, Harvest Bible Chapel.

To my friends for life: Maura, J, Norrie, Annie, T.

To my tribe, the people who have always loved me unconditionally: Phil, Maggie, Ben, Alice, and Betty.

To my two sons. Blessed are the pure in heart (Matthew 5:8), and blessed are the merciful (Matthew 5:7).

To the love of my life, Joe. You're still, always, my favorite person to be with.

To God, who wrote my favorite Book (Jeremiah 15:16).

.

ABOUT THE AUTHORS

Gary Chapman is the author of the #1 *New York Times* bestseller *The 5 Love Languages,*® a speaker, and a counselor. Gary's passion is to help people form lasting relationships. He has the uncanny ability to hold a mirror up to human behavior, showing readers not just where they go wrong, but also how to grow and move forward. Gary travels the world presenting seminars, and his radio programs air on more than 400 stations. For more information, visit 5LoveLanguages.com.

Paige Haley Drygas has worked in book publishing since 1999. She was the General Editor of *True Images: The Bible for Teen Girls* and *True Identity: The Bible for Women*; helped develop *The Extreme Teen Bible* and *Revolution: The Bible for Teen Guys*; and contributed to the *Extreme Teen* line of books, which has sold more than one million copies. She has partnered with authors Nancy Leigh DeMoss, Priscilla Shirer, and Tammy Maltby. In her former life, she taught high school English at Wheaton Academy and coached soccer. She is the President of Peachtree Editorial Services and lives with her husband and two sons in Peachtree City, GA.

NOTES

1. Proverbs 18:21.
2. Proverbs 15:1.
3. Acts 20:35b.
4. John 13:1b.
5. John 13:12b, 14–15.
6. R. J. Palacio, *Wonder* (New York: Alfred A. Knopf, 2012), 71, 120.
7. Psalm 68:6.
8. Exodus 20:12.
9. Jeremiah 17:9.

STRENGTHEN YOUR RELATIONSHIPS
ONLINE

Discover your love language for free

Explore resources and tools

Locate LIVE events

Listen to podcasts

Share your story

Watch videos

Get free stuff

www.5lovelanguages.com

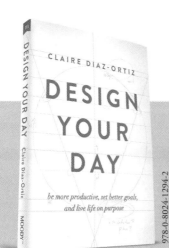

Productivity guru Claire Diaz-Ortiz introduces a productivity and goal-setting model that will help you do more in less time and succeed more often. Whatever is on your to-list, she'll help you choose smart goals and put strategies in place to achieve them.

978-0-8024-1294-2

Paul Angone has compiled 101 secrets for twentysomethings—secrets concerning work, relationships, and life. This humorous book will help equip you to live with confidence and wisdom in your post-college years.

978-0-8024-1084-9

Also available as ebooks

THE BETTER LIFE

small things you can do right where you are

CLAIRE DIAZ-ORTIZ

978-0-8024-1293-5

In winsome style, Claire Diaz-Ortiz coaches readers with vignettes from the odd and common corners of her life. A top-level Twitter employee, world traveler, author, and mom, she shares stories and insights on balance, productivity, rest, and other essentials for making your life a little better every day.

MOODY
Publishers

From the Word to Life